SCHOLASTIC

Differentiating
Assessment
in the Reading Workshop

Karin Ma & Nicole Taylor

New York • Toronto • London • Auckland • Sydney
Mexico City • New Delhi • Hong Kong • Buenos Aires

Teaching *Resources*

For my family, both at home and in my classroom.

–KM ✏

To all the students who have inspired me throughout the years. Keep up the great work! Thanks to my greatest love, Sanáa, and her "Abby."

–NT ✏

Editor: Sarah Longhi
Content editing: Sarah Glasscock
Cover design: Brian LaRossa
Interior design: Kelli Thompson
Illustrations: Maxie Chambliss

ISBN-13: 978-0-545-05397-6
ISBN-10: 0-545-05397-8

1 2 3 4 5 6 7 8 9 10   40   15 14 13 12 11 10 09

Contents

All featured forms are available on the companion CD.

Introduction

Conferring—Unlocking the Power of Assessment

"Teacher feedback through conferences is essential; teachers need to let children know when they've used a strategy correctly, encourage them to share their thinking with the teacher and their peers, challenge them to think out loud about how using the strategy helped them as a reader, and correct misconceptions when they occur."

DEBBIE MILLER, (2002) READING WITH MEANING: TEACHING COMPREHENSION IN THE PRIMARY GRADES

Conferring appears to be an arduous task, but it doesn't have to be. As teachers, we talk to our students all day long and guide them on the path to success. By adding some structure to these interactions, we can make our work with students more effective. And when we create a system like the one we present in this book, with clear procedures for conferring and maintaining accurate and detailed assessment notes, we are able to better assist our students and ensure that their writing reaches its full potential.

Listed below are some of the many questions we've heard from teachers about conferring.

- How will I be able to meet with so many children?
- When can I make time to meet with my students?
- What do I say?
- What should I teach them now?
- How do I organize my notes—and what do I do with them?
- What will my other students do while I'm conferring?
- How can I make sure students will follow through on the skills I have taught them?
- How can I differentiate my conferences to meet all my students' needs?
- How can I use these notes to communicate with the school community?
- Why should I confer anyway?

All of these questions will be addressed in the upcoming chapters, with the aim of helping you put this new assessment system into practice in your own classroom.

How This Book Developed

We met as new kindergarten teachers in the fall of 2001 as we were about to embark on the school year in a brand-new school in New York City. The moment we met, we formed an instant bond. We had similar teaching styles, the same enthusiasm for learning, and high expectations for ourselves and our students. We quickly discovered how difficult managing a primary classroom is—in addition to planning a reading and writing curriculum that met and challenged all students. To support one another, we met frequently outside of the classroom to share what we were teaching and plan for the upcoming months. We still maintain this practice today.

A few summers ago, we thought to ourselves, "How about developing a system of conferring that could really work in the classroom?" We had tried several different conferring systems in the past, but none ever worked as we had envisioned. Some of our first systems for taking notes involved many sheets of loose-leaf paper that were frequently lost, as well as notes jotted haphazardly in notebooks that we never looked at again. We even tried using sticker labels that we were supposed to make notes on during the reading workshop and then transfer over to student record sheets. After a couple of months, these stickers ended up staying right where we left them. Everything was time-consuming and inefficient. We felt that our students deserved more, and so did we. Why confer at all if it wasn't helping us plan instruction and improve student work?

We wanted to develop a system for conferring that would enable us to take notes quickly so that we could spend more time teaching. It was always difficult to decide quickly what deserved a compliment and which skills to teach students. We thought that having a reference at the top of our conference notes showing the skills we expected students to master during the unit would help us decide what to say during a conference. By thinking ahead of time about unit goals and objectives, we would have a better plan for each individual conference. We could even differentiate for each reader's needs.

Our Reading Conference Notes sheets helped us develop the method that we've come to depend on—assessment, planning, and instruction through conferring. By creating a conference note sheet for each unit, we realized that we could track lesson and unit goals. Everything we needed for reading conferences and even small group work would be right there. It would take the guesswork out of conferring, and it was a simple, yet effective way to confer!

Standards-Based Instruction and Conferring

When we began to implement the workshop model in our classrooms, we quickly realized that we could easily help our students meet—and often exceed—all the city and state standards through this approach to instruction. The inclusion of these standards—at each grade level—is a cornerstone of each unit of study that helps us to differentiate instruction and assessment.

The following is an overview of the New York State literacy standards and how we align them with our reading instruction:

- **Standard 1 requires students to read for information and understanding.** According to the standard, "students will collect data, facts, and ideas, discover relationships, concepts, and generalizations; and use knowledge generated from oral, written, and electronically produced texts." Through studying and reading nonfiction, students are able to achieve this goal.

- **Standard 2 requires students to "read and listen to oral, written, and electronically produced texts and performances, relate texts and performances to their own lives, and develop an understanding of the diverse social, historical, and cultural dimensions the texts and performances represent."** Students learn how to make connections to texts during read-aloud and shared reading, and through these connections, they better understand what they're reading.

- **Standard 3 requires that students "analyze experiences, ideas, information, and issues presented by others using a variety of established criteria."** Students are best able to accomplish this task through partnership time, book clubs, and whole-class discussions of read alouds.

- **Standard 4 requires that students "use the social communications of others to enrich their understanding of people and their views."** Whole-class and partner "turn and talk" discussion structures afford students many opportunities to hear differing viewpoints and to debate ideas.

With careful planning, the reading workshop helps us maintain standards-based instruction. From this planning work, we help you take efficient and purposeful conference notes to keep track of how well your students are progressing toward meeting these standards and to differentiate your planning in light of these assessments.

How to Use This Book

Throughout this book, you will explore different scenarios you may have encountered in your classroom. These scenarios will prepare you for anything you might face the next time you confer. Sample conferences, mini-lessons, and strategy group lessons are sprinkled throughout the chapters to help you picture what your workshop might look and sound like. Reading Conference Notes sheets are filled in to showcase how this new system of conferring can work for you. Although every classroom is unique and there are so many different kinds of students, we've attempted to help you differentiate your instruction to help meet all their needs. For instance, we've included English language learner (ELL) tips throughout this book. Here is how the book is laid out.

Chapter 1 offers an overview of conferring. You will gain insight into what the parts of a conference are, how conferring can be a useful assessment tool in your classroom, when you should do it, and how to stay organized.

Chapter 2 explains exactly how to take conference notes effectively and efficiently to collect exactly the data you need. We suggest several options for how to take your notes so you can choose which way works best for you. Common concerns about how to organize and manage your new assessment system will be addressed.

In **Chapter 3**, we show you how conferring fits into nine units of study that we use each year to cover our curriculum and meet state literacy standards. You can decide which units you'd like to teach—or how to adapt our ideas to your own units—and when to teach them. You will come across many work samples for grades K–2 so you can see how authentic conferences help support a primary reading curriculum. These samples highlight ongoing work, as well as celebrated response pieces. They reflect students of varying abilities, as well as children learning the English language. Sample conference note sheets help you visualize what the system will look like when you begin to use it. We provide examples of literature we love to use during these units, as well as different celebrations we've successfully tried in the past.

Chapter 4 provides portraits for students of differing ability levels as they progress through the year. We closely examine students in grades K–2 and paint a picture of how these children are likely to begin the school year. This will help you get started with reading workshop and help you know what to expect and the best way to reach students during conferring time. Conference note sheets help illustrate these expectations.

The strategies in **Chapter 5** give you a better grasp of organization, as well as planning. Conference notes are sometimes difficult to compile and look at collectively, so this chapter shows you how to use checklists to inform your future instruction, whether it's individual, small-group, or whole-class.

Chapter 6 discusses how to use assessment data from your conferences to better communicate within your school community about student progress. Improving communication with parents, teachers, administrators, as well as students, will ensure children's progress continues throughout the school year. Utilizing your conference notes sheets effectively can help convey any concerns you have for students within your classroom.

How to Use the Companion CD

Like most teachers, we love to get tools that help simplify our lives. We wanted to make sure our readers would have the tools they need to implement this method of taking conference notes. The companion CD contains customizable versions of all the conferring and planning forms shown in this book, which are also available as reproducible pages in the Appendix (pages 105–143). In this way, you may photocopy the reproducible form or print it from the CD and fill it in by hand, or you may fill in the digital form, print it, and save the digital file to update—in fact, you may want to create an assessment folder on your hard drive for each child. You can record your students' names, the date, and quick, targeted notes that become an organized part of each student's record.

The ideas and tools presented in this book will help ensure your success this school year and in the future. You will feel much more confident about your ability to maintain assessment records and how to use them to make instructional decisions in your classroom.

Tip

To customize and save the files on the CD, you will need to download Adobe Reader™, version 7.0 or higher. This download is available free of charge for Mac and PC systems at www.adobe.com/products/acrobat/readstep2.

Chapter 1

Conferring—101: Basic Tools to Make Assessment Work

"I almost feel like there should be bells ringing and lights flashing as I describe my assessment notebooks. For without a doubt, they're my most important teaching tool."

SHARON TABERSKI, (2000) ON SOLID GROUND: STRATEGIES FOR TEACHING READING K–3

As a teacher, you want to portray yourself as a reader. You maintain your own reading folder and produce reading responses similar to the ones you expect from children. The students come to view you as a fellow reader—and not simply a reading teacher. The most important aspect of this relationship is the conversation that happens between two readers. This trust that develops will help you confer effectively within your classroom and take quality assessment notes. Your assessment notes truly help drive your instruction.

In this chapter you'll learn more about the following topics:

- What are the parts of a conference?
- How should I decide what to teach the readers in my class?
- How can conferring help me as a teacher?
- When is the best time to confer?
- How can I use reading partners effectively?
- How can I stay organized?

How Is a Conference a Conversation?

At the start of the school year, you want to create an inviting tone so your students feel like they are active participants in the conferences you have with them. Conversations require that at least two people speak and that back-and-forth dialogue is what you want to start in September.

Productive conversations imply that you are a great listener, and that skill starts with you, the teacher. By listening closely to what your young readers have to say, you can identify and research their needs, and begin the important assessment work of conferring. A conference is a tool that teachers can use to help assess their students and inform their instruction. Research is one of the most important parts of conferring. It requires that teachers step back and look to see what their class is doing to first determine what individual students might need.

In the following example, you'll see how Mr. M, a second-grade teacher, uses conferences with his students.

Mr. M understands the importance of establishing the reading workshop. He knows the reading level of each child and has set up everyone with a just-right book bag (a large plastic resealable bag.) He has assessed all his students using running records so that he has a baseline for each reader in his classroom. As the year moves forward, Mr. M will use this baseline to determine how well each student is progressing. He'll continue to take running records regularly throughout the school year so he can make sure that all students will meet their reading goals by the end of the school year. These running records give Mr. M a window into the minds of his young readers because he notes what types of errors they make, as well as whether they self-correct and how well they retell and show fluency and expression. This background information is vital in guiding conferences. Some schools pass along a running record or other information from the previous year's teacher to the present one. This information provides valuable insight into each reader. (See page 12 for more information on Informal Running Records.)

Now, through conferring, Mr. M can start getting to know each individual reader's strengths and weaknesses. He gains key insight into which student to meet with first when he takes a few minutes to look around the classroom to see who might need additional support and as he glances at his conferring notebook. Mr. M takes out a new Reading Conferences Notes sheet and writes Tony's name on it.

Watch as Mr. M begins his conference with Tony.

Mr. M: Tony, what book are you reading today?

Tony: *George and Martha.* I love this series!

Mr. M: Oh, you've read books about George and Martha before?

Tony: Yeah, I even read *George and Martha Round and Round.* George and Martha are very best friends!

Mr. M: Wow! You know a lot about these characters already. Can you read a little bit of the story to me?

(As Tony begins to read, Mr. M jots down his observations in the "What reader can do" column of the conference note.)

Mr. M completes his research, which consists of looking at what Tony is doing, speaking with him about his reading, and listening to him read a portion of the text. Now it's time to give Tony a compliment and decide what to teach him next. Mr. M looks over his conference notes from the first unit he taught, Launching the Reading Workshop, and picks one aspect of Tony's reading work to highlight.

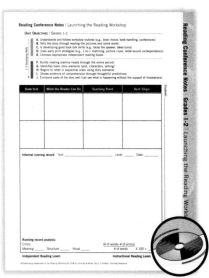

Reading Conferences Notes Sheet, Grades 1–2
Print From CD/Copy From Appendix, page 106 (Find reproducible conference sheets for nine units of study and blank templates, pages 105–123)

Mr. M: Tony, you are such a smart reader! You know who the characters in this book are, and you realize what a good friendship they have! That's really going to help you understand what's going on in the story.

(Mr. M has been thinking about all the possible teaching points for this conference. Glancing at the unit's objectives on the conferring sheet, he sees that he could give Tony some prompts to use during partner talk (C) or help Tony make smart predictions using his knowledge of this series (I). Since Tony has shown a great interest and knowledge about the series, Mr. M decides to work on objective I. He hopes working on making predictions will bolster Tony's comprehension skills for future readings in different series.)

Reading Conference Notes | Launching the Reading Workshop

UNIT OBJECTIVES | **GRADES 1–2**

1–2 Developing Skills

A. Understands and follows workshop routines (e.g., book choice, book handling, conferences)
B. Tells the story through reading the pictures and some words
C. Is developing good book talk skills (e.g., faces the speaker, takes turns)
D. Uses early print strategies (e.g., 1-to-1 matching, picture clues, letter-sound correspondence)
E. Chooses appropriate independent reading books

F. Builds reading stamina (reads through the entire period)
G. Identifies basic story elements (plot, characters, setting)
H. Begins to retell in sequential order using story elements
I. Shows evidence of comprehension through thoughtful predictions
J. Envisions parts of the story well (can see what is happening without the support of illustrations)

Date/Text	What the Reader Can Do	Teaching Point	Next Steps	
9/17/07 George and Martha Level L	A, B, D, D, F, G (char.)			Student: Tony

Mr. M's notes about what Tony can do.

Mr. M: Tony, I want to teach you something that will help become an even better reader. While we read, it's important for us to stop and predict what's going to happen. You know so much about George and Martha's friendship. We can use that information to help make a smart guess about what will happen next when we're reading.

Tony: Oh.

Mr. M: Watch me as I read a part from "Story Number One: Split Pea Soup." Notice how I stop and predict what will happen next because I know about their special friendship.

(Mr. M begins to read page 8, where George is unsure of how to get out of eating Martha's split pea soup.)

Mr. M: Okay, I'm going to stop here. George hates drinking Martha's split pea soup, but he says how hard it is to tell her. It is difficult breaking that kind of news to your best friend. I don't think George will tell Martha he hates the soup. He doesn't want to hurt her feelings.

(Mr. M reads on and learns that he's right: George tries to get rid of the soup without telling Martha.)

Mr. M: Oh, look. I knew it! George didn't tell Martha. He loves her too much!

Tony: Yeah, look where he put the soup—in his shoes. That's funny!

Mr. M: Now you can try to make your own smart predictions using what you know about their friendship.

(Mr. M turns to "The Last Story: The Tooth." He selects this part knowing it has a good place to stop and make a prediction. Tony begins to read.)

Tony: Oh, George is hurt. I think he's going to find his friend Martha. She's helping him.

(Tony reads on and confirms his prediction.)

Mr. M: You're doing a great job predicting, Tony. Remember to do this in every story you read.

As you see, Mr. M completes his conference with the teaching point he selected. He clearly states what he wants Tony to do. Then he models the teaching point and instructs Tony to try it himself. Mr. M frequently restates the teaching point so that Tony will remember it, and reminds him of it at the end of the conference. Knowing the George and Martha series well helped Mr. M make good choices to assist Tony during the conference. It's important to be familiar with the books your students are reading, especially any series that is popular in your classroom.

THE PARTS OF AN EFFECTIVE CONFERENCE

Most of your conferences will sound similar to the one Mr. M had with Tony. You begin by researching the class and student, deciding what the student does well, complimenting him or her, deciding on your teaching point, and teaching the specific unit objective. Always remember to restate the teaching point throughout the conference to ensure your students will know what to do. Use consistent language in your mini-lessons, as well as in your conferences. Choose your words wisely. Be aware. Think: *Will my students understand what I mean*? The conference notes sheet will help you figure out which goal to focus on. It is also a great way to keep track of your conference.

GETTING TO KNOW YOUR READERS: EARLY ASSESSMENTS

Conferences help you get to know your students well. In September, you can use several forms to assess the readers in your class.

Meet Our Readers Interview Sheets

"Meet our Readers" interview sheet will give you a better picture of the kinds of readers in your classroom. We've included an interview sheet for levels K–1 (top right) and a more advanced one for levels 1–2 (bottom right).

The K–1 interview sheet can be given to your youngest readers. The picture support will help them fill it out. You may also wish to send it home for parents to help their child fill it out.

The 1–2 interview sheet provides even more information about the readers in your classroom. Gifted first graders and second-grade students benefit from filling out this detailed interview sheet. You might even pair readers in your classroom and have them interview one another. They can work on their listening and questioning skills while getting to know one another at the start of the school year. Sheets like these help build the reading community in your classroom.

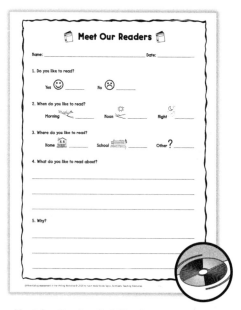

Meet Our Readers K–1 Sheet
Print From CD

Meet Our Readers 1–2 Sheet
Print From CD

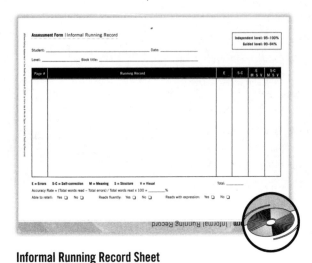

Informal Running Record Sheet
Print From CD

Informal Running Records: Building a Baseline

In order for you to make the most of your conferences, students need to be reading books at their instructional level as soon as possible. Start the first week of school with a concerted effort to take a running record for every child within the first two weeks of school, and then repeat the process periodically throughout the school year. Running records are done periodically throughout the school year to determine if a child needs to move up a level for independent reading. Have a sample book for each level at which you plan to assess the readers in your class ready at your conference nook. Also have your Informal Running Record Sheets ready to fill out. You can type in the text on the customizable form so the data is easier to record, or you can simply make a checkmark for each word read. The accuracy rate you get for each reader will help you figure out at which level your students can begin their reading venture.

In addition to a student's ability to decode words, he or she must read with comprehension, fluency, and expression. A quick check of comprehension can be done by asking students to retell the text when they finish reading. At the bottom of the Informal Running Record, note their ability to retell. As your students read, take note of the smoothness of their voice, as well as their tone. Use your discretion when determining a level for each reader in your class. A student may read a text with 100% accuracy, but it may still be too difficult if he or she cannot understand the text.

September Reading Checklist

Another great way to get started with your reading workshop is to use the September Reading Checklist, which helps you quickly note whether students are practicing important reading behaviors during independent and partner time.

By walking around the room for a couple of days with this checklist in hand and observing students, you can assess how your students are handling the basic routines. The information you collect will allow you to differentiate instruction to meet the needs of each student. If you notice the whole class is struggling with a specific skill, you can reteach this skill during a whole-class mini-lesson. However, if only a handful of students are struggling with a basic routine, you can remediate through small-group instruction.

Assessment Form | September Reading Checklist

Students	Independent Reading Routines					Partnership Routines				
	Turns pages appropriately	Holds book right side up	Is able to choose books	Puts book back properly	Sits in reading spot	Sits with partner	Has one book out at a time	Takes turns reading	Says something about the book	Stays engaged in reading

September Reading Checklist Sheet
Print From CD

Why Confer?

Conferring is at the heart of the reading workshop. It provides insight into your students' present success while informing future instruction. Praise is a powerful motivator for any child. The compliments you will give during conferences make children feel confident in their abilities as readers; they are often unaware of the things they are doing well while they are reading. And because reading becomes a silent activity in first grade, it can be difficult for you to know exactly what a child is doing. Conferences provide an opportunity to do the necessary research that will keep the readers in your classroom on the right path.

ASSESSMENT AS A MOTIVATOR

As a teacher you strive to meet the individual needs of all your students. Conferences can be a special time of the day for you to get to know your children. They come to expect your help and look forward to the next conference. Taking time to speak with each child lets him or her know that they are important to you. This helps build a special community in your classroom. Children gain the necessary confidence to succeed in this risk-free environment. They are confident readers.

The following example shows how a first-grade teacher, Ms. S, effectively uses conferring to motivate her students.

It's late September, and Ms. S is still having difficulty getting her first-grade readers to use quiet voices, although she has taught them to use one-inch voices when reading to themselves. When Ms. S confers with Dominique, who is effectively reading with a one-inch voice, she gives the student a compliment on following this routine (A). She makes sure she says the compliment loud enough for nearby students to hear it. Sure enough, other readers begin to remember to use a one-inch voice as well. After Ms. S gives the compliment, the classroom becomes much quieter. She realizes the power of her words and plans to compliment other children about their quiet reading in the days that follow. Over time, these compliments will help the class become proficient quiet readers. A quiet classroom makes conferencing easier.

ASSESSMENT DRIVES INSTRUCTION

Your assessment of each student will help you make future instructional decisions. Conference notes become a useful guide to lesson planning within your classroom. When you confer again with a student, it's helpful to glance at your notes before making any decisions. Looking back at a previously noted teaching point is the starting point for your research.

The sample conference below illustrates how a teaching point for Tony leads to a compliment when Mr. M notices that Tony has followed through with the skill. If Tony had not demonstrated the skill, Mr. M would need to reteach it. Conference notes help Mr. M differentiate instruction for Tony. This close monitoring ensures that Tony will become a successful reader.

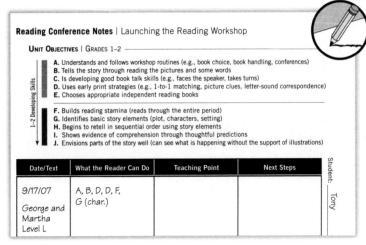

Mr. M uses his conference notes to compliment Tony on his mastery of making predictions.

Mr. M: Tony, I notice you're reading a new George and Martha book.

Tony: Yeah, Mr. M. This one's great. George is acting just like he always does. Look, I was able to guess what George was going to do next.

Mr. M: Can you show me?

(Tony reads a part of the book and demonstrates effective prediction-making.)

Mr. M: Wow! You remembered what I taught you about predictions! Great job!

(Mr. M looks over the "Next steps" column to focus on a new teaching point.)

Mr. M: I'd like to teach you how you can talk about this book with your reading partner. A great way to get started is by telling your partner something you notice about the character in your book. You can start by saying, "I notice . . ." Watch me try that with our class read-aloud, *Poppleton in Winter*.

(Mr. M opens up the book to Chapter 1, "Icicles.")

Mr. M: I remember what happens here. Poppleton has icicles hanging around his house, and all his friends keep telling him to take them off. Listen to me as I tell you something I notice about the character Poppleton. I notice . . . Poppleton is very stubborn. He won't listen to anyone.

(Mr. M points to Tony's book.)

Mr. M: Now you try it! Read a few pages and be ready to say one thing you notice about George or Martha to your reading partner.

(Tony starts reading. During partner time, Mr. M hears Tony tell his reading partner, "I notice Martha is such a good friend." He's pleased that Tony is using the discussion prompt that he learned.)

Conferring will benefit you and your students in so many ways. It helps create a climate of caring and responsible citizenship. Children know you will check to make sure they are following through on what you've taught them to do. As a result, their reading will improve tremendously throughout the school year.

When to Confer?

Conferring is done daily after your reading workshop mini-lesson. (For more information on reading workshops, see Chapter 2.) Give students a few minutes to settle down. These precious moments also give you a chance to assess how successfully they follow the routines. Be sure to scan the room for behavioral concerns. These observations will help you develop teaching points regarding the workshop routine for future conferences. You may also wish to take the time to look back at your conferencing notes to ensure that you're prepared.

WHO NEEDS YOU THE MOST? PRIORITIZING YOUR CONFERENCE SCHEDULE

Conferences are crucial to your students' success, but they can be time-consuming. In order to meet with as many students as possible in a period, you will need to strategize, taking into account the different needs of your students. You may want to confer with certain children more often than others. Consider the readers in your class. English language learners and struggling readers may need to meet with you more frequently to ensure their reading stays on course. Any child whose promotion is in doubt needs additional conference time and small-group time so you can maintain records showing you've done everything possible to allow this student to meet grade-level standards.

Our | Classroom Notes

In our experience, English language learners need additional support during reading workshop. One way we give students this support is by pulling them aside for small-group work. For instance, we conduct content-based studies to help build their vocabulary. This group work helps when it's time to read on their own. By listening to additional read-alouds, ELL students are gaining the oral language that's important for the reading work they'll be doing. Some read-alouds include books we plan to read to the whole class later in the week. Hearing these stories first gives English language learners the background they need so they won't be lost during the whole-class read-aloud.

We also reread big books that these students are familiar with so their confidence is increased, and we preview big books before we read them to the whole class so we can introduce unknown vocabulary and sentence structures. We've noticed that ELL students often choose to read familiar big books, use a pointer, and act out the stories during center or choice time. They like to pretend that they are the teacher and ask one another questions. This confidence comes from hearing the story so many times.

If any English language learners are about to read a new series, we always confer with these children first to give them background about the series. Telling them about the characters, setting, and any other important information prepares them to read the series.

As you get used to using conferring notes, you'll cut your conference time in half. You will discover the best way to take notes effectively and how to use your previous assessments quickly to help you decide what to teach, which gives you more time to meet with more students. An average conference should take five to eight minutes.

SCHEDULING THE READING WORKSHOP IN YOUR SCHOOL DAY

There are several times a day in which you might like to plan your reading workshop. This important decision determines when you will conduct your reading assessments. You want to make the most out of your conferring time so choosing a time of day that works for your classroom is crucial. Take a close look at your individual class to see what part of the day works best for you.

When children walk in first thing in the morning, they are alert and may have lots of reading stamina. Morning workshops help settle the class down. After lunch and recess can be opportune times for reading workshops as well. Reading tends to be a calming activity and allows children time to wind down.

FLEXIBLE SCHEDULING

You can choose to organize your conference schedule in many different ways. If you like to have complete control over which students you'd like to meet with on a regular basis, try assigning a conference schedule in which each table meets with you on a different day of the week. Posting a clear chart like the one below serves as a visual reminder to students. This also prevents children from constantly asking, "When are you conferring with me?"

Day	Student Names (Readers)
Mon.	Justin, Kai, Shania, Caroline, Sane
Tues.	Tommy, Rita, Rebecca, Onterio
Wed.	Vicki, Jason, Brian, Steven, Wendy
Thurs.	Sarah, Eric, Billy, Jennifer
Fri.	Nancy, Matthew, Yancy, Xin Yi

When Will You Conference With Me? sheet posted in classroom

For more flexibility, you can choose on the spot which students to meet with. Moving around from table to table helps with management. This is especially useful for kindergarten and first-grade students. Your mere presence at a particular table helps the students stay on task.

Alternatively, you may choose to confer with readers at various reading levels in a given day. Some teachers find it easier to meet with readers who are all at the same reading level. This schedule can help you stay focused with the challenges that these readers are facing.

In order to promote more independence in your reading workshop, you may want to create a conference sign up sheet like the one shown on page 17. You will still have an opportunity to meet with students of your choosing, while allowing for student ownership. It's more challenging to keep track of all the students in your class with this system, but students will usually keep you informed if they are having trouble reading their books and/or trying out the skills you've taught them. This kind of schedule works best with second-grade students or a more mature first-grade class because they often know when they need help with their reading. To keep track of which students you met with during the course of a month, you can use a Conference Dates Checklist. Record the names of the students who signed up for a conference with you at the end of the day.

| Conference Sign Up Sheet |
Please help me! |
Mon.	3/24/08	① Vicki	② Matthew
Tues.	3/25/08	① Nancy	② Rita
Wed.	3/26/08	① Xin Yi Feng	② Shahia
Thurs.	3/27/08	① Sarah	② Brian
Friday	3/28/08	① Jason	② Tommy

Conference Sign Up Sheet posted in classroom

PEERS AS MENTOR READERS: A BUDDY SYSTEM THAT WORKS

It's difficult to meet with all the students in a class often enough to ensure that they're reading every book successfully. Some students may have questions about the text that could be answered if they worked with a reading buddy. Partnerships play a crucial role in your reading workshop. Every day, after reading independently, children will have partner time. Sometimes they'll read with their buddies, who may help with decoding work, while in other sessions, they may focus on book talk. This partnership helps develop students' comprehension of texts.

After a mini-lesson, students read independently first and then join their partners. These meetings can be arranged in many ways, and may change throughout the school year. You may find it best to allow students to choose a reading spot anywhere around the classroom, which can help limit the excessive noise when they're reading since they're spread throughout the room. And children always find little nooks and crannies in which to read: Some students

Look at your informal running records and your conference notes to help you pair readers of similar abilities—it's important that these buddies are at the same reading level. Note that these partnerships will change throughout the school year.

Create and display a chart showing which students are reading buddies.

prefer to read at their desks, while others enjoy lying on the carpet or a sofa. Pillows placed strategically around the room can also create a comforting environment. When partner time arrives, one partner leaves his or her reading spot and joins his or her partner to read and talk.

Another option is for students to turn their chairs and sit back to back with their reading partners. This encourages more independence. When you signal that it's time for partners to work together, students simply turn their chairs next to each other and squish together like "peanut butter and jelly" to begin their partner read.

Nicole's | Classroom Notes

In my kindergarten classroom, students' reading stamina is limited at the start of the school year. I like to increase their reading time by creating shorter increments of independent and partner reading. For example, during a unit of study on concept books, I let my children do independent reading back to back in their concept books, followed by partnership time with their concept books. Then we switch to independent reading with the emergent storybooks in their plastic bags, followed by partner time with these storybooks. The children love this and read for much longer periods of time without even realizing it. This allows me time to confer with many more students and pairs during the reading workshop!

ELL Tip

English language learners require special consideration in the classroom. Proficient speakers can be paired with ELLs so they get additional support. It's also a good idea to create a buddy group involving three students so the English language learner can hear other children speak and will not feel pressured to communicate if they are uncomfortable about doing so. Pairing an English language learner with a proficient student who has a native language in common with the ELL is also beneficial.

OTHER GROUP SETTINGS THAT HELP READERS GROW

There are many other opportunities for reading work to be done throughout the school day, and other crucial components to a successful reading workshop are shared reading, guided reading, strategy reading groups, read-alouds, literacy centers, and word work.

In shared reading, an enlarged text is used to demonstrate a variety of reading skills and strategies. Some of these texts highlight different genres so your readers can learn what each genre looks like and how to read it.

Guided reading groups consist of a small group of students who have similar reading levels, which allows you to pinpoint a specific reading skill you want children to practice while you guide them through a text. This process involves an introduction to the text, an understanding of the challenges students may face, and questions to support them through the text. As you conduct your guided reading groups, the other students in the class are engaged in work at well-planned literacy centers.

A strategy reading group is similar to a guided reading group except that students may not necessarily be reading the same text or on the same reading level. Therefore, the reading skills or strategies you emphasize in this group are much more general.

Read-alouds are texts you choose for a variety of reasons. You may use read-alouds to spotlight a particular genre, introduce a character in a series, or to enjoy the storyline or your love for a particular author.

As you conduct your guided reading groups, the other students are usually engaged in work at literacy centers. These centers incorporate learning activities that reinforce the work you're doing in your classroom, so they must be well thought out in order to help support all the readers in your class. Activities can take the form of alphabet/sight-word bingo, a poetry center, a big book center, tape-a-story, or reading the room.

Word work is a time to focus on phonics by teaching children different word-solving skills. This activity can be done as a whole class, in partnerships, or through individual assignments.

Tools for Organizing and Preparing for Your Conferences

At first glance, taking and organizing your conference notes can seem overwhelming, but we've created some support forms to help you organize and locate information efficiently. A Class Checklist sheet of the unit objectives helps streamline and organize the data you've collected from your conferences. On this form, you can see the ongoing progress of the class as a whole.

We include a Class Checklist sheet for each unit of study. The skills that students are expected to achieve by the end of unit appear at the top of each checklist. Underneath the skills, there is a space to record which skills your students mastered.

There are many ways to successfully use these checklists. You may wish to check off the mastered skills directly after conferring with a student. This way the newly mastered skill is fresh in your mind. Another way is to look back at your confer-ence note sheets on a weekly basis and fill in the newly mas-tered skills. (Chapters 2 and 5 will give you a better picture of how to use these checklists in your classroom.)

At a quick glance, the checklists provide you with insight into how you and your class are doing. The sample second-grade checklist on page 20 from Mr. M's class shows how it will look by the middle of the Launching the Reading Workshop unit.

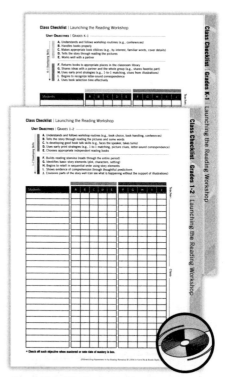

Class Checklist for Launching the Reading Workshop, Grades K–1 and 1–2

Print From CD/Copy From Appendix, pages 124 and 125 (Find reproducible checklists from nine units of study and blank templates, pages 124–142)

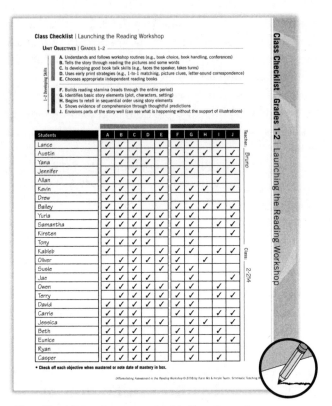

Class Checklist as it appears about halfway through Launching the Reading Workshop unit.

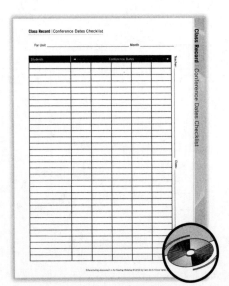

Conference Dates Checklist
Print From CD/Copy From Appendix, page 143

The record of student mastery helps you make smart teaching and assessment choices. In Mr. M's case, since most students in the class have a checkmark under skill B (tells the story through reading the pictures and some words), he no longer needs to reinforce this skill in future lessons, although he will continue to monitor and support Jennifer, Kirsten, and Kaleb in individual conferences. When he realizes that most of his students do not have a checkmark below objective H, Mr. M decides to create several mini-lessons supporting that skill. And he plans to pull a handful of students into a small-group strategy lesson to work on objective F.

Because it can be difficult to ensure that you've met with every student several times during the course of a unit, we find that a Conference Dates Checklist is another good tool to use.

A simple list with students' names and spaces to check off every time you meet with these students helps ensure that you've met with every child before starting the cycle over. You may wish to record dates rather than use check marks so you know how long it's been since you've met with each student.

After a full week of conferring, you may feel as if you've met with the whole class, but sometimes this is not the case. Children

Class Record | Conference Dates Checklist

For Unit __Print Strategies__   Month __November__

Teacher: Bruno   Class: 2-214

Students	Conference Dates				
Lance	11/7	11/14	11/21		
Austin	11/7	11/14	11/22		
Yana	11/7	11/15	11/26	11/29	
Allan	11/9	11/16	11/26		
Kevin	11/8	11/15	11/23		
Drew	11/7	11/14	11/27		
Bailey	11/7	11/9	11/19	11/22	
Yuria	11/7	11/16	11/19		
Samantha	11/15	11/20	11/27		
Kirsten	11/7	11/10	11/15		
Tony	11/9	11/14	11/18		
Kaleb	11/8	11/11	11/17		
Oliver	11/6	11/13	11/22		
Susie	11/6	11/15	11/26		
Jae	11/5	11/11	11/18		
Owen	11/16	11/12			
Terry	11/7	11/14	11/26		
David	11/12	11/16			
Carrie	11/5	11/9	11/14		
Jessica	11/10	11/14	11/18		
Beth	11/15	11/10	11/19		
Eunice	11/11	11/17			
Ryan	11/5	11/9	11/14		
Cosper	11/11	11/15			

Differentiating Assessment in the Reading Workshop © 2008 by Karin Ma & Nicole Taylor, Scholastic Teaching

Completed Conference Dates Checklist for unit called Print Strategies.

may have been absent or away from their seat on the day you conferred with their table. Therefore, it's important to keep track of the students you confer with daily so you have weekly assessments on each child. This way, if Allan was absent on Monday, the day for his conference, you'll notice a check missing beside his name at the end of the week, and make a mental note to meet with him another day. This list can also be enlarged and posted as a chart so that older children can put a checkmark by their names after a conference. This will cut back some paperwork time for you.

Conferring is an important assessment tool in your classroom, and all your record-keeping sheets, including the individual conference note sheets and the class checklist sheets, will help you keep accurate, detailed, and informative assessment notes for each child in your classroom. It is up to you to decide how to implement this system in your classroom so that it best suits your students' needs. In the next chapter, we'll take a closer look at how this system may work in your classroom and how it may fit within your reading workshop.

Chapter 2

How Is It All Done?

"Every teacher knows that the climate of the classroom is a critical element in children's learning and that classroom tone is set during the first days and weeks of school. I've learned that the entire tone of the year can be determined by the care, time, and effort I invest at the beginning."

CAROL AVERY, (2002) . . . AND WITH A LIGHT TOUCH: LEARNING ABOUT READING, WRITING AND TEACHING WITH FIRST GRADERS

Once you establish reading workshop in your classroom, you will see that it follows the same principles every day. The workshop becomes routine, and this routine helps keep the readers in your class on track. Your conferences will become short mini-lessons for individual students, and you will be able to differentiate your instruction so that all the readers in your classroom can succeed. Again, your conference notes will help you differentiate effectively.

In this chapter you will find out more about the following questions:

- How does conferring fit within the reading workshop model?

- How are a mini-lesson and a conference similar?

- How can I begin to confer for the school year?

- How do I take my conference notes?

- How can I differentiate my objectives for different grade levels and abilities?

- What are some common problems I might encounter?

- How will I manage my reading workshop effectively?

Conferring in the Reading Workshop Model

We follow a basic workshop model in which conferring is one of three components:

1. Mini-lesson
2. Conferring/small-group work
3. Share time

Every reading workshop begins with a mini-lesson, and then students go off to read independently. During independent reading, you have the opportunity to differentiate instruction by either conferring on an individual basis, conducting a small-group strategy lesson, or working with a guided reading group. Students will then have partner reading time where they read books or have book talk. In second grade, you may have some students meet with a book club, a small group that reads the same book or books within the same series. At this time, you have another opportunity to conduct conferences or small group work. Reading workshop concludes with share time where you celebrate the reading successes of the day.

Nicole's | Classroom Notes

In order to build reading stamina in my kindergarten classroom, I plan my workshop structure differently based on each unit of study. Occasionally, children may have the opportunity to do independent and partner reading twice! These sessions are broken down into smaller amounts of reading time. For example, during my nonfiction unit of study, I have students read nonfiction books from tabletop baskets for about seven minutes independently and then spend five minutes reading and talking about these books with a reading partner. Next, I let children read just-right leveled books from their reading book bags for about seven minutes, followed by five minutes of partner time. This helps improve their reading stamina and allows me to confer with many more students during workshop time—and my students don't even realize how long they've been reading!

THE MINI-LESSON

The mini-lesson is your teaching time. Since it often sets the tone and provides skill and strategy tips that you will use in a conference—and because the mini-lesson structure is similar to the conference structure—it's useful to review how it works. Every mini-lesson begins with a connection that sets a purpose for the reading that day. This may be a connection to the ongoing reading work you're doing or a compliment about students' reading achievements. Next you teach the reading goal. This can be done in several ways. You can show examples, demonstrate, have students model (fishbowl-style) or use texts.

After teaching the reading goal, you invite students to actively participate by trying the skill or strategy right there in your meeting area so you can provide additional support before they go off to work independently. Young readers can then envision what their reading work will look like for that day. The mini-lesson ends with a link to reading time: a reminder of the teaching point.

There are many kinds of learners in every classroom and it's important to consider ways to appeal to a range of learning styles when students are actively engaged in applying a new skill or strategy. (You should try out a variety of active engagement tactics during your conferences. Looking over past assessments of the children in your classroom, will give you a good picture of the kind of learners you are conferring with. This information enables you to differentiate the active engagement tactics to meet students' needs, as well as keep each child interested and engaged. A chart with pictures, for example, serves as a support for your visual learners. Tactile learners benefit from turning the pages of their own copies of a text to locate examples of print strategies, like high-frequency words or compound words. Auditory learners gain a lot from turn-and-talk time. Acting out scenes from their books helps sensory learners.

One mini-lesson can turn out in so many different ways, depending on the way you choose to differentiate. For instance, as you begin a new unit on building comprehension, you may choose to start with a lesson teaching children to retell the story related in the text. The active engagement portion of the lesson may look different in many different classrooms.

For visual learners, you may have children use picture cards to put the story in sequential order. Tactile learners benefit from using finger puppets to retell a story. For sensory learners, have children act out the beginning, middle, and the end of the story with their whole body, including gestures and facial expressions.

A Mini-Lesson in Action

Mr. G is a first-grade teacher with 25 children in his class. The children are enthusiastic about reading time, and they've been building up their stamina. Mr. G would like to begin to develop his students' book talk. He decides to start with a mini-lesson involving simple retelling since many students are struggling with retelling an entire story. (You always start the mini-lesson with a connection. It puts students in the mind frame for reading workshop and helps them reflect on what they've been learning in reading.)

> **Mr. G:** Remember how we've been reading the big book, *What's Cooking?* I know you guys love to tell each other the ending of the story when the class gets pizza. Well, readers can tell all the parts of a story.

(By pinpointing what students are struggling with, Mr. G sets up the purpose for the mini-lesson. This helps students anticipate a learning strategy that will help them with this goal. Mr. G follows with a clear teaching point.)

> **Mr. G:** Today I'm going to teach you that good readers show they understand a story by retelling the beginning, middle, and end of it. Watch me as I use my fingers to retell all the parts. (Mr. G retells what happens in *What's Cooking?*, holding up a finger for beginning, middle, and ending events.)

Mr. G: Did you see how I retold the story? Remember—we know all the parts of the story, not just the ending. I want you to try it! Remember *The Snowy Day?* We've read that book a lot! I want you to turn and tell your partner the beginning, the middle, and the end across your fingers. Get ready!

(It's important to clearly state the teaching point in kid-friendly language and then model what you'd like students to do. This procedure sets up children to successfully complete the active engagement portion of the lesson. Using texts children are familiar with makes the lesson go smoothly, too.)

Mr. G: I heard Madison tell Emily all the parts of *The Snowy Day.* Madison remembered what Peter did in the beginning, the middle, and the end of the story. She put up one finger for each part. So boys and girls, remember that today you'll retell the story that you read before you choose another one to read. You can also practice retelling the story during partner time, like we just did!

The link summarizes the lesson and reminds students what to do before you send them off to read independently. To prevent confusion, it's essential to use consistent language every time you restate the teaching point.

Conferring/Partner Reading and Small-Group Instruction

After the whole-class mini-lesson ends, children are sent to read on their own, while the teacher differentiates instruction further through conferences and small-group work. Children's reading stamina will grow throughout the year based on their grade level, and as their stamina grows, you'll have more time to consult your conference notes and differentiate instruction.

Keep in mind that the conference and small-group lesson follows the structure of the whole-class mini-lesson. The teacher chooses a skill for children to work on, demonstrates it, and then has them try to use that skill in their reading.

Share Time

The end of the reading workshop is signaled by share time. You may want to have two quick shares: one at the end of independent reading time and the other at the end of partner time. Share time can be organized in a different way each day. Occasionally, you may invite volunteers to read parts of their books and showcase their successes based on your conferences with them. Additionally, you can choose to share something "smart" that students have done. For instance, you may have partners sit together and model for the whole class the "smart" reading work they did or they may model book talk. This is a special time of the day that all children look forward to. The readers take pride in their accomplishments and often gain insights into future reading work. The class offers comments, questions, and suggestions regarding the books they read.

Conferring the Right Way

In order for conferring to run smoothly and be a success in your classroom, you need to set up a system that students understand and is easy for you to use. It's important to start off the year right so you will have many opportunities for individualized instruction based on your student assessments. Below we show how Ms. C starts off her year.

It's the start of the second week of school and the reading workshop has been set in motion. Ms. C's first graders are enthusiastic about reading after she's talked it up so much for the first week of school. The students know how important reading is to Ms. C. It's her favorite time of the day. The students have begun to follow the routines and rules without prompting during workshop time. Now, Ms. C feels it's time for them to understand that she'll be conducting conferences and what they will be expected to do during a conference.

In addition to preparing a chart to go along with her lesson, Ms. C has also invited a former student, Vivian, who is now in second grade, to come and help teach the first graders what a conference sounds like. Vivian is excited to help out the new first graders learn the ropes. Inviting a former student to show students the structure of a conference is a useful strategy. Children tend to listen to other children, especially older students, and they will act out what they see. This strategy works for introducing children to peer conferring as well. Listen in as Ms. C begins her lesson on basic conference structure and procedures.

Ms. C: Boys and girls, we are so lucky to have a special expert in the room today to help us understand conferences a little better. Let's welcome Vivian to class 416.

Class 416: Good morning, Vivian!

Ms. C: We've been learning all about how to start our reading. We've gotten to know where the book baskets are located in the classroom. Today, we're going to learn another part of reading workshop. Conferences are a special time for me to get to know you as a reader. Today I'm going to teach you what you should do when I have a conference with you. Watch and notice what Vivian does while I confer with her.

(Ms. C sets up her lesson for the class. She begins to model what a good conference sounds and looks like. She has spoken to Vivian in advance to ensure that the lesson goes smoothly. Ms. C sits quietly next to Vivian as she begins her reading. She takes a few moments to research the reader in front of her.)

Ms. C: What are you doing today, Vivian, in your reading?

(Vivian takes a minute to think and looks at her book.)

Vivian: Reading about the girl and her friends.

Ms. C: Can you read a little bit for me?

Vivian: "Sally went to play with Emma. 'Can I climb up?' she said. 'No, you can't,' said Emma. 'Go away, Sally.'"

Ms. C: Oh, no! That's not what good friends should say! I liked how you slid your finger across the words as you read, and you didn't skip any words. Good job! Today I want to teach you how you can sound mean, just like Emma talked to Sally.

Vivian: Okay!

(Ms. C rereads the passage, sliding her finger across the words, with greater character expression.)

Ms. C: Did you hear how I sounded mean just like Emma did? Now you try it.

(Vivian reads over the page and imitates Ms. C.)

Ms. C: So remember, when you want to sound just like the character, read again to sound like they would sound.

(By showing your class what a great conference looks and sounds like, children learn quickly what to do. Through this method, you've set the tone for your conferring for the rest of the year. Ms. C turns her attention to the students in her class.)

Ms. C: Did everyone see what Vivian and I did during our conference?

Class 416: Yes!

Ms. C: Take a minute to think about what you saw. Tell your neighbor two things we did well.

(The class quickly turns to talk to one another. Ms. C actively listens to several partners. She pulls out a chart like the one pictured below to show the class some of the things they mentioned.)

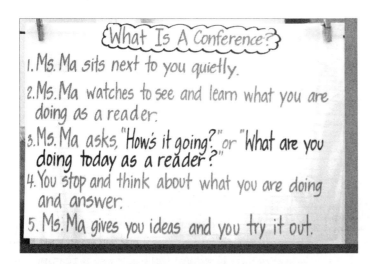

This chart is a good tool for students to refer to when they are not sure what to do. Remember when making your own chart to use language that is commonplace in your classroom. Choose words that you use consistently and that you expect the children to use as well.

Ms. C: Remember, I'm going to walk around and confer with several of you. If you forget what to do, you can look at the chart and remember what Vivian did. Off you go to read.

This kind of mini-lesson is the best way to get your reading conferences started on the right track in your classroom. Remember that students will need several reminders about routines and strategies they must practice independently, especially if they are not used to the workshop model.

Karin's | Classroom Notes

I always keep my charts simple. I make the sentences short and add a lot of picture support to help my first graders remember what the key words mean. I have a lot of English language learners in my classroom each year, and the pictures really help them understand the charts better. I often see children walk over to the charts and read them during workshop time. This helps them build greater independence and ownership of their work.

Record Keeping

Your conference notes sheets are a place for you to record helpful information for your future reading mini-lessons. You'll notice in the example below that the specific unit objectives are listed clearly at the top of each sheet. (Blank Reading Conference Notes templates for K–1 and 1–2 are available on pages 122 and 123 and on the CD.) You may customize this form to reflect the goals of your own units of study.) Whether you choose to use the Reading Conference Notes sheets we include or whether you design your own, make sure that the unit objectives are listed accurately and reflect your goals and students' needs. The more familiar you are with the unit objectives, the more efficiently you are able to confer.

Each time you meet with a student, record the date, the title of the book they're reading, and its level so you can keep track of what level he or she is reading. In the notes shown here, it's easy to see that Jacob consistently is reading level B books.

Next record the skills that the student has mastered. Write a compliment you've given to the student under "What the Reader Can Do." Don't hesitate to compliment

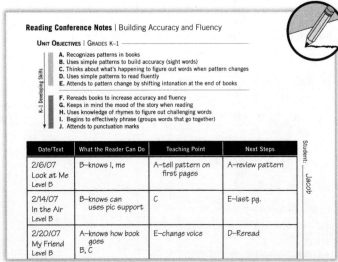

Sample Reading Conference Notes sheet for Building Accuracy and Fluency unit.

students on the same objectives several times since this will encourage them to continue the smart reading work they're doing. After you've chosen an objective to teach, document it under the Teaching Point column. The objective may change from conference to conference or stay the same. Record the objectives you'd like to delve into the next time you meet with the student, note it under the Next Steps column. Looking at the information in this column can help you choose a teaching point for the next conference, which will save you a lot of valuable teaching time.

Remember to make notes short and concise. At first, you may wish to simply jot down the letter(s) that correspond to target objectives in the appropriate boxes. As you become more familiar with note taking, you may choose to write more elaborate notes. Keep in mind that the objectives at the top of the sheet list general goals you want your children to achieve. You may be more specific about the objective in your note taking, as the example at right shows.

In this example, the teacher uses letter symbols to record objectives E, F, I, and J, but she adds specific information to her notes as well. For example, on November 1, Kaitlyn was able to pay attention to the illustrations and the pattern (A–D) of *Before I Go to School*, which helped her read accurately. The teacher chose to work on the intonation of Kaitlyn's reading (E).

The teacher takes notes quickly and efficiently by using the letters for the objectives, as well as abbreviations.

To save time, you may choose to use shorthand as you make notes. It's helpful to have a system of abbreviations in place such as attends (*att.*), reads (*rds.*), and different (*diff.*). This system needs to work for you consistently and feel natural.

Another quick and easy system for note taking is to check off or circle each objective when it's mastered. A quick look at the top of the conference notes sheet will give you a good indication of how the student is doing in the unit. If all the objectives are circled or checked off, mastery is complete, and enrichment is an option. As the sample conference notes sheet on page 30 (top left) shows, Jocelyn, a gifted first grader, is clearly ready for some second-grade challenges. Her teacher can move on to grades 1–2 unit objectives (F–J).

Your goal is to guide all students toward mastery by the end of the unit for the specific grade level. If nothing is circled or checked off by mid-unit, extra attention should be given to this student. More information about how to use your notes to help you support remediation or enrichment of a particular skill appears in Chapters 4 and 5.

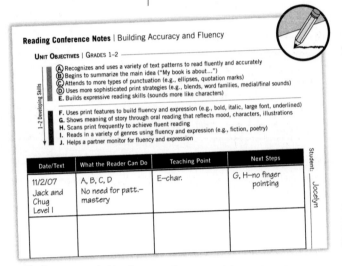

Reading Conference Notes | Building Accuracy and Fluency

UNIT OBJECTIVES | GRADES 1–2

Ⓐ Recognizes and uses a variety of text patterns to read fluently and accurately
Ⓑ Begins to summarize the main idea ("My book is about...")
Ⓒ Attends to more types of punctuation (e.g., ellipses, quotation marks)
Ⓓ Uses more sophisticated print strategies (e.g., blends, word families, medial/final sounds)
E. Builds expressive reading skills (sounds more like characters)

F. Uses print features to build fluency and expression (e.g., bold, italic, large font, underlined)
G. Shows meaning of story through oral reading that reflects mood, characters, illustrations
H. Scans print frequently to achieve fluent reading
I. Reads in a variety of genres using fluency and expression (e.g., fiction, poetry)
J. Helps a partner monitor for fluency and expression

Date/Text	What the Reader Can Do	Teaching Point	Next Steps
11/2/07 Jack and Chug Level I	A, B, C, D No need for patt.– mastery	E–char.	G, H–no finger pointing

Student: Jocelyn

Circling mastered objectives can give you a quick overview of a student's progress.

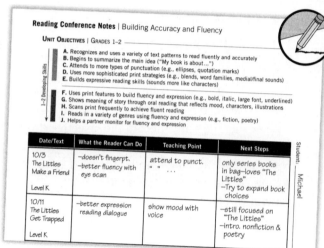

Reading Conference Notes | Building Accuracy and Fluency

UNIT OBJECTIVES | GRADES 1–2

A. Recognizes and uses a variety of text patterns to read fluently and accurately
B. Begins to summarize the main idea ("My book is about...")
C. Attends to more types of punctuation (e.g., ellipses, quotation marks)
D. Uses more sophisticated print strategies (e.g., blends, word families, medial/final sounds)
E. Builds expressive reading skills (sounds more like characters)

F. Uses print features to build fluency and expression (e.g., bold, italic, large font, underlined)
G. Shows meaning of story through oral reading that reflects mood, characters, illustrations
H. Scans print frequently to achieve fluent reading
I. Reads in a variety of genres using fluency and expression (e.g., fiction, poetry)
J. Helps a partner monitor for fluency and expression

Date/Text	What the Reader Can Do	Teaching Point	Next Steps
10/3 The Littles Make a Friend Level K	–doesn't fingerpt. –better fluency with eye scan	attend to punct. " " . . .	only series books in bag–loves "The Littles" –Try to expand book choices
10/11 The Littles Get Trapped Level K	–better expression reading dialogue	show mood with voice	–still focused on "The Littles" –intro. nonfiction & poetry

Student: Michael

These detailed notes will help remind the teacher to nudge Michael toward nonfiction and poetry during his next book-shopping time.

On the other hand, you may want to expand your note taking by adding more details to provide greater insight into the needs of children in your classroom. The conference note above shows that second grader Michael is building his expression when he reads books with a lot of dialogue, however, the teacher also records her concern about Michael's limited book choice and how to address it.

DIFFERENTIATING YOUR OBJECTIVES

Teaching reading can be difficult in any heterogeneously-grouped classroom. Children come to you from a variety of literacy backgrounds. Some may have begun reading at an early age, while others have never picked up a book before starting kindergarten. Therefore, it's important to differentiate your lessons and conferences to meet the needs of all the readers in your room.

To ensure that the objectives on the Reading Conference Notes sheets match the needs of all your learners, we've differentiated the unit objectives accordingly. Every unit has a sheet listing objectives geared for grades K–1, and one listing objectives appropriate for grades 1–2. Some key objectives repeat or are modified for particular grade levels. Select the best sheet to use based on grade level and the needs and strengths of readers in your classroom. If, for example, most of the first graders in your room are reading higher leveled books/series, then you would use the sheets for grades 1–2. The shaded bars beside the objectives help highlight the progression of skills your readers should acquire: light shading for grades K, medium shading for grade 1, and dark shading for grade 2.

On the Grades K–1 Reading Conference Notes sheet, objectives A–E represent skills that are the easiest to master. Most kindergarten students should be able to master them by the end of each unit. The next tier of skills, objectives F–J, are slightly more difficult, and first graders should be able to attain these skills by the end of a unit. On the Grades 1–2 Reading Conference

Notes sheet, objectives A–E are suited for on-level first graders, while objectives F–J show what second graders should be able to accomplish by the end of a unit. Be sure to carefully consider which sheets are more appropriate for your students. The skills listed build upon one another—and they help you differentiate to meet the needs of your students.

Karin's | Classroom Notes

When you have a classroom consisting largely of English language learners, you must also alter your conference notes sheets to reflect their reading levels and abilities. Oftentimes, my binder is filled with conference sheets that are further differentiated to suit each individual learner. I organize my notes so that below-level learners were sectioned off from the on-grade level or above-grade level learners. This makes my conferring time more efficient. Meeting with readers on similar levels helps me stay focused. By having my conference notes arranged in this manner, I'm better able to cater to the needs of my students.

COMPILING YOUR CONFERENCE NOTES

There are many ways you may choose to compile all your conference notes. For instance, you may print out sheets that correspond to the number of students in your class and bind them into a conferring notebook.

These conference note sheets are bound together in a book format.

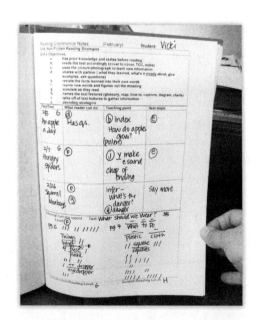

These conference note sheets have been placed in a folder to make them easy to transport around the room. You may also prefer to arrange the notes on a clipboard and rearrange them as you meet with students each day.

Management

Well-designed management is crucial to the success of any conferring system. Children need to learn what is expected of them during independent reading time so they can rise to the challenge of reading on their own. Starting in September, you'll need to have a clear system of routines in place, including the following:

- How to keep students on task
- What to do while the teacher is conferring
- How to get help when the teacher in conferring
- Where to confer
- How to keep your conferring materials accessible

It is important to teach children how to work independently. Visual signals help remind students of what they need to do. Early in the year, teach hand signals for bathroom and water, such as a thumbs-up. At the start of the school year, many children will attempt to interrupt your conferences. It's imperative that students refrain from interrupting conference time. One way to prevent this from happening is to wear a conference necklace with a note or picture that indicates you're busy. Anytime a child comes near hold it up as a reminder that you cannot help him or her at that moment. Another way to manage your students is to hold up a stop sign. Students will quickly learn this means "stop, think, and go back to work."

Our | Classroom Notes

It is crucial to explicitly teach the routines and expected behaviors for reading workshop. By consistently and repeatedly reviewing these routines, children become responsible and independent readers. Our conference time goes much more smoothly as well.

To help students meet our expectations, we role-play different scenarios that can occur throughout reading workshop. Students take the role of the teacher, while we play the part of a student, acting out humorously exaggerated behaviors. The children are usually very entertained by our antics as we become the most disruptive readers in the classroom. Although it's funny, the demonstration shows students how important it is to follow the rules of reading workshop. As the year progresses, we highlight positive reading habits by having students who demonstrate these habits share what they did at the end of the workshop. This is often the best way to prepare students for working with a partner.

These readers show the class what good partnerships look and sound like.

Students also need to learn that there are other teachers in the room—all their peers. Wearing or posting a sign that reads "Three before me!" tells children that they are responsible for themselves. They should ask three students for help before coming to you. When students are stumped by a word or have a question about a story, they can ask their partner for help later. You can show second graders how to write their questions on sticky notes or flag tricky words in the book so they can refer to them during partner work.

This conferring nook allows the teacher to stay in one spot with all the assessment tools.

Another aspect of management is where to conduct your conference. A conference corner (shown at right) can be a place in the room where students come to meet with you. The advantages of having this nook are that you can store your materials in a central location and you can stay in one place rather than walking around the room. This often saves time.

On the other hand, moving from table to table lets children know that you are nearby, and your presence may help prevent behavioral problems. So you may opt for a conference stool that is easy to carry around (bottom left). Another benefit of having a portable seat is delivering your teaching to other students at the table where you hold a conference. While you are at a table conferring with one student, all the children at the table can benefit from listening in on your conferences. This way, you will reach many more children during the reading period.

It is important to have all of your conferring materials handy. A conference caddy (bottom right) can contain your conference notes, some sample leveled books for taking running records on the go, a personal book bag filled with favorite texts to use as models for your conferences, familiar read-alouds, guided reading books for the week, sticky notes, a white board (for decoding strategies), a dry-erase marker, an eraser, and any other tools you feel you need.

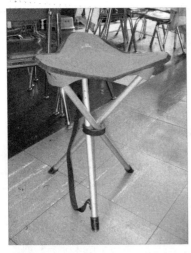

This conference stool is lightweight and easy to carry around.

A conference caddy helps to keep you organized while you conduct your assessments.

We have tried out many different seating arrangements for reading time. Sometimes we allow children to choose their own reading spots around the classroom. We make a big production out of students picking their private spot. Once students have learned the routines, this becomes a celebration in the classroom. We speak about places we like to read at home. Some children name their couch, bed, or even the bathtub! They decorate an index card showing themselves reading in their nook, and we tape it to their spot. This helps us and the students keep track of where they belong for reading time. During partner time, they decide which spot to share. We often hear students saying, "Do you want to sit in my spot today?"

Every year, we encounter readers who cannot choose a good reading spot for themselves and need our help. Sometimes, we give them a choice between two spots—special places in the room that are easily visible wherever we go, and far away from other distractions.

When teaching kindergarten, we find that it's best to limit the amount of movement around the room. This prevents additional noise during workshop time. We have students sit back-to-back for independent reading time. They can do this seated in their chairs or on the floor. Sitting back-to-back cuts out a lot of talking between children and allows for quick transition time. When it's partner time, students turn their chairs or bodies side by side.

Other routines students will need to master include book shopping schedule, book bag maintenance, and the reading noise level. A great resource for tightening up the routines in your classroom is Kathy Collins's *Growing Readers: Units of Study in the Primary Classroom* (2004).

Students take turns sharing their reading nooks.

Sitting back-to-back is a helpful way to provide structure for kindergarteners during independent reading time.

By designing a system for your conferences, you'll show your students what is expected of them and they'll behave accordingly. It's important to think about all the aspects of management discussed above before the school year begins so you can immediately teach the system to your students. In doing so, you will better be able to assess students regularly and keep track of those assessments. In the long run, you'll spend less time going over rules and routines and be able to focus more time on enhancing your students' reading.

Chapter 3

Looking Closely at the Units of Study With a Focus on Assessment

"I do want teaching to be child-centered and responsive, and yet I also believe we benefit from anticipating possible areas of emphasis that our entire class room community can rally around."

LUCY McCORMACK CALKINS, (2001) *THE ART OF TEACHING READING*

Throughout the school year, you will expose your readers to various genres. With each genre come distinct goals to master. Your conference note sheets will cater to the characteristics of each genre (or other unit focus) as well as to the needs of each individual learner.

In this chapter you will find answers to the following questions:

- What are some possible reading units I might teach this year?
- What are my goals for each unit?
- What are some good read-alouds I might use?
- How can I celebrate my students' work for this month?
- How can I support the English language learners in my classroom?
- What might my students' reading and thinking sound like for each unit of study?
- How should my conference notes look?

Reading Units K–2 Overview

Kindergarten through second grade, students generally read in the same genres, and these genres become the topics of many of our units of study. However, we differentiate the goals of each unit to meet the needs of the readers in a particular grade. On the conference note sheets we've included in this chapter, the unit objectives at the top of each sheet are listed in a continuum of developing skills.

This continuum goes from the least complex skills to the most difficult skills. Therefore, as children progress through the primary grades, they should be able to achieve all the skills on the conference note sheets. Students will study the same reading skills, and repetition is very important if these readers are to become successful. Some reading skills that students will practice are envisioning, predicting, decoding, retelling, inferring, summarizing, making connections, critiquing, questioning, developing theories, and accumulating the text. Their ability to use these skills will improve as they progress through the grades.

As we discussed in the Differentiating Your Objectives section in Chapter 2 (pages 30–31), the conference note sheets are designed by grade level (grades K–1 and grades 1–2) so that differentiating assessment is even easier to do. Again, each child will demonstrate varying levels of ability. Referring to your conference notes sheet for each unit tells you what type of skills children should be able to master. This will give you insight into how each student is progressing through reading workshop. For example, second graders who are only succeeding in skills A–E might need extra support, whereas kindergarteners who master unit objectives A–E might need a challenge. The unit objectives will translate into mini-lessons that you teach, as well as conference teaching points and small group lessons. These objectives will guide your instruction during the unit. This allows each child to acquire new skills in his or her own time. This is why flexible assessment forms like the leveled conference notes we've designed are so helpful.

There are many different units to choose from, and we've selected nine that best support our students' growth and meet our district and state standards: Launching the Reading Workshop, Print Strategies (Just-Right Books), Building Accuracy and Fluency, Building Comprehension, Building Your Book Talk, Nonfiction Reading Strategies, Character Investigation, Reading Centers, and Shared Reading Texts. You choose which units you'd like to delve into, as well as the most appropriate time of year to teach it. Again, always consider your grade level, the reading abilities of the children in your classroom, and the materials you have available. Before the start of the school year, make a plan that outlines the units you'd like to teach and when you'd like to teach them. This plan will help you organize your library appropriately.

As a culmination of every reader's work and mastery of skills, each unit ends in a celebration—and each unit should be celebrated in a different way. Children become excited about the celebrations and take pride in their work. They know they are growing as readers and will want to showcase this growth. Units generally last about one month. It's good practice to plan ahead of time when your celebrations will take place. These "deadlines" make your readers feel like they are working towards a goal. They know they will have an audience to show what they've been learning. You may wish to note the celebrations at the start of the month on your class calendar. If you plan to invite parents or other guests, be sure to provide celebration dates in your school calendar or class newsletter.

Launching the Reading Workshop

As you launch the reading workshop at the beginning of the school year, children are learning the workshop rules and routines and how to handle books. Students who have taken part in reading workshop in previous years will learn the expectations for the workshop quickly so they can move on to comprehension work, especially those in second grade. You may want to focus your mini-lessons on some or all of the skills outlined in the Launching the Reading Workshop conference notes sheet (see page 38). As always, consider the needs of the children in your class when deciding on your mini-lessons.

For each unit of study, you should have a couple of mentor texts to read aloud to prepare children for the unit and to use during conferences. These texts are valuable tools for highlighting different reading strategies you want students to try. You can also read aloud these stories to prepare for any writing work you want students to do. It's important to choose texts that match the focus genre and theme of the unit.

At the start of the school year, choose read-alouds that have to do with school and adjusting to a new classroom, teachers, and friends. The following mentor texts can help ease students' initial concerns about a new classroom: *Countdown to Kindergarten* by Alison McGhee, *The Kissing Hand* by Audrey Penn, *Wilson Sat Alone* by Debra Hess, *First Day Jitters* by Julie Danneberg, and *Will I Have a Friend?* by Miriam Cohen. Some fun read-alouds about school are *David Goes to School* by David Shannon, and *A Fine, Fine School* by Sharon Creech. Additionally, you may want to read some books that will get children excited about reading and choosing a good reading spot, including *Carlo Likes Reading* by Jessica Spanyol, *The Best Place to Read* by Debbie Bertram and Susan Bloom, and *A Quiet Place* by Douglas Wood.

Throughout each unit, and regardless of which grade you teach, you'll take conference notes. As the sample on page 38 shows, second grader Lizzie begins the year reading books that are too difficult for her. She understands the basic concepts of print, like how to turn the pages in the book (A), however, she doesn't know how to choose just-right books (E). Lizzie would also benefit from future work on retelling (H) and using the pictures to help her retell (B).

Within this first unit, it's beneficial to have two celebrations. When you begin the year with lots of routines and expectations of reading workshop, the readers in your classroom may lose sight of the purpose of reading. Two celebrations will help keep the momentum going in your classroom. For the first celebration, consider throwing a library "grand opening" after you've completed your assessments. At the end of the unit, you might celebrate all the reading habits students have learned this month by having them illustrate one reading routine they can do well. They can share these with the whole class or just a reading partner.

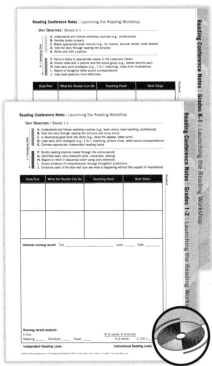

Objectives for Launching the Reading Workshop Unit, Grades K–1 and 1–2
Print From CD/Copy From Appendix, pages 105 and 106

ELL Tip

At the start of the school year, English language learners may need a lot of additional support during reading workshop. A great way to provide this support is through the read-aloud *Carlo Likes Reading* by Jessica Spanyol. Each page in this book shows the giraffe, Carlo, reading the names of common objects found in different places. The labels in this book help build content vocabulary that these students will need to know.

Furthermore, you can model appropriate reading behaviors for ELL children by using simple directions and pantomime. For example, state, "turn the page" and pantomime the action. You may also want to create a chart listing the reading behaviors you'd like to see in the classroom with photographs of students acting out each behavior.

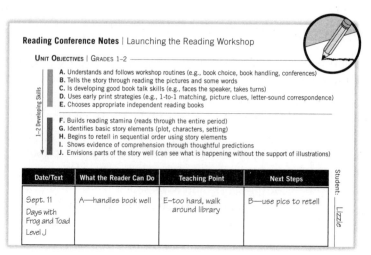

Reading Conference Notes | Launching the Reading Workshop

UNIT OBJECTIVES | GRADES 1–2

1–2 Developing Skills

A. Understands and follows workshop routines (e.g., book choice, book handling, conferences)
B. Tells the story through reading the pictures and some words
C. Is developing good book talk skills (e.g., faces the speaker, takes turns)
D. Uses early print strategies (e.g., 1-to-1 matching, picture clues, letter-sound correspondence)
E. Chooses appropriate independent reading books

F. Builds reading stamina (reads through the entire period)
G. Identifies basic story elements (plot, characters, setting)
H. Begins to retell in sequential order using story elements
I. Shows evidence of comprehension through thoughtful predictions
J. Envisions parts of the story well (can see what is happening without the support of illustrations)

Date/Text	What the Reader Can Do	Teaching Point	Next Steps
Sept. 11 Days with Frog and Toad Level J	A—handles book well	E—too hard, walk around library	B—use pics to retell

Student: Lizzie

At the beginning of second grade, Lizzie is reading level J books.

Our | Classroom Notes

We always start the year with a big library grand opening. This initial ribbon-cutting ceremony gets parents and children excited about reading. Before we introduce the class library to the students, we decorate the bookshelves with ribbons and streamers. Outside the classroom door, we hang student-created flags that display the titles of their favorite books. Students get to take turns cutting the ribbons with giant plastic scissors to symbolize the opening of our library. Everyone always cheers when the ribbons are cut. Getting parents involved early on sets the tone for the year. Parents are invited to come shop for books with their children, and they will be more likely to come in for future celebrations. It also shows parents how much fun reading to their child can be!

Students eagerly cut the ribbon for the library grand opening.

Print Strategies (Just-Right Books)

It's important for children across all the grades to study a variety of print strategies. These strategies often build upon one another and become more complex as books increase in difficulty. Good readers use a variety of strategies to decode words and can usually use the strategies flexibly.

This unit should be done in conjunction with helping children locate and read "just-right books" (books at their independent reading level that require no teacher support). The readers in your classroom will begin to develop more stamina for reading as they practice a variety of print strategies. This print work starts with a focus on using illustrations, repetitive text, sight words, and initial consonants to figure out challenging words. As students become more competent readers, they will learn how to monitor for meaning by checking if what they are saying as they read sounds right and makes sense. They will also be better able to choose just-right books for independent reading. Partners will help each other decode words, as well as begin to talk more about the books.

We find it helpful to display charts during this unit of study to illustrate the reading strategies children are learning to use. These charts serve as reminders of the lessons you've taught them, and you can refer to them during future mini-lessons and conferences.

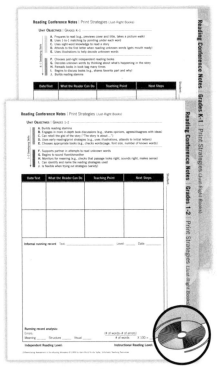

Objectives for Print Strategies (Just-Right Books), Grades K–1 and 1–2
Print From CD/Copy From Appendix, pages 107 and 108

This picture-supported pocket chart reminds students of reading strategies to use before, during, and after reading a book.

ELL Tip

Making sure English language learners have appropriate leveled books is very important. They may need to start out at lower levels than the rest of your students, but they'll eventually catch up to the other readers in your classroom. Other ways to support your ELLs include the following:

- Using early readers with patterned text to reinforce basic sentence structure
- Focusing intensely on sight-word recognition to build a reading word bank
- Conducting group lessons on target skills like final sounds and suffixes, alphabet recognition, and letter sounds
- Having children retell using story language in books or sketching the beginning, middle, and end of the story in their reading notebooks

During this unit, you should read many big books and model the decoding strategies you're teaching. (As we mentioned earlier, you'll find it practical to carry around smaller copies of these big books to use during your conferences.) You may also model strategies with any leveled books that match the levels of the readers in your classroom. These texts can be enlarged to chart-size or put on the overhead for whole-class work. Some excellent fiction big books for this unit are *I Went Walking* by Sue Williams, *In the Tall, Tall Grass* by Denise Fleming, *Silly Sally* by Audrey Wood, and *Crunchy Munchy* by Brenda Parkes. Joy Cowley has also written many wonderful big books for the primary grades, including *Hairy Bear; To Town; Dan, the Flying Man*; the Meanies collection; and the Mrs. Wishy Washy collection. A good book of poetry for this unit is *Morning, Noon, and Night: Poems to Fill Your Day* by Sharon Taberski, and a terrific choice for nonfiction is *Beavers* by Helen H. Moore.

Another excellent way to model these reading strategies is through large, laminated photo cards, such as the *Reading with Strategies* cards from Celebration Press (2008). Each card contains a colorful photo and simple matching sentence. The cards also have cling-ons to cover up words or parts of words for decoding work. This set of cards can be used during whole-class mini-lessons or small group work.

As the example below shows, Jessie, a kindergartener, is beginning to read leveled books. She's excited about reading and tries out anything the teacher shows her. After a lesson on "getting your mind ready to read" by looking at the cover, Jessie successfully tries the strategy on her own (A). She also has a good base of sight words and can recognize them in print (C). However, Jessie is having difficulty tracking the words with her finger and occasionally says more words out loud than are printed on the page. She could benefit from focusing on 1-to-1 matching (B), using the initial consonant (D), and using picture support (E).

Danny, an advanced second-grade reader, is reading books in the Cam Jansen series by David Adler. He enjoys independent reading time and is engrossed in the books he's reading. Danny is successful in meeting almost all the first-grade objectives (A, C, D, E), as well as a second-grade objective (G) as shown in the conference note on page 41. However, when it's time for partner work, he resists discussing the books with his reading partner. A good teaching focus would be to encourage Danny to talk more about the books and to give him prompts he can use with his partner, such as "I love when . . ." or "Do you know how I can figure out this word?" (B, F).

This Print Strategies unit allows children to become more self-aware about how

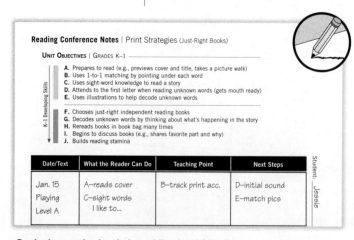

Beginning reader Jessie is tackling level A books.

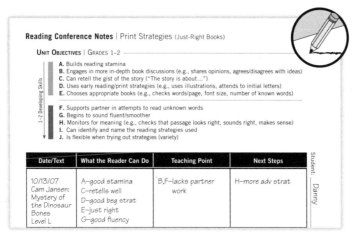

Reading Conference Notes | Print Strategies (Just-Right Books)

UNIT OBJECTIVES | GRADES 1–2

A. Builds reading stamina
B. Engages in more in-depth book discussions (e.g., shares opinions, agrees/disagrees with ideas)
C. Can retell the gist of the story ("The story is about…")
D. Uses early reading/print strategies (e.g., uses illustrations, attends to initial letters)
E. Chooses appropriate books (e.g., checks words/page, font size, number of known words)

F. Supports partner in attempts to read unknown words
G. Begins to sound fluent/smoother
H. Monitors for meaning (e.g., checks that passage looks right, sounds right, makes sense)
I. Can identify and name the reading strategies used
J. Is flexible when trying out strategies (variety)

Date/Text	What the Reader Can Do	Teaching Point	Next Steps	Student: Danny
10/13/07 Cam Jansen: Mystery of the Dinosaur Bones Level L	A–good stamina C–retells well D–good beg strat E–just right G–good fluency	B,F–lacks partner work	H–more adv strat	

Future lessons for Danny might include work with more complicated word-solving strategies (H)

"word smart" they are. They're able to name the reading strategies they use, and they look forward to telling you excitedly which ones they tried out when reading a new book. Have children showcase these reading strategies through your classroom celebration. Their "reading bag of tricks" has grown, and they are better able to juggle all the strategies at once.

One celebration idea is to ask children to help you graph the reading strategies the class uses by jotting a strategy on a sticky note and pasting it on a grid. At the end of a specified reading period, children can see how many strategies they've used and determine which are the most popular.

Partners celebrate what they've learned at the end of the Print Strategies unit.

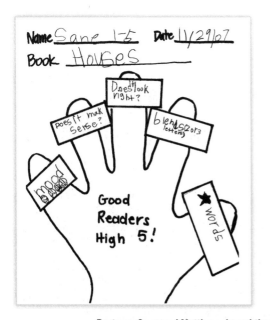

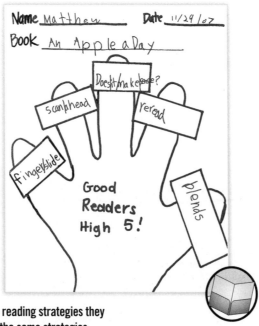

Partners Sane and Matthew shared the five reading strategies they use, and they discovered they use some of the same strategies.

Another celebration possibility is the "reader's high five." Students trace their hands and name five decoding strategies they use, one per finger. After sharing these with a partner, pairs give each other a high five in celebration of their great reading work!

To celebrate what they've learned in this unit, children can also name the reading strategies on a simple chart titled "I Have Word Power."

These three first graders were able to pinpoint the strategies they used to help decode tricky words in their books.

Objectives for Building Accuracy and Fluency unit, Grades K–1 and 1–2
Print From CD/Copy From Appendix, pages 109 and 110

Kindergarteners may simply wish to read a story to a classroom partner or a family member, which shows and celebrates their growth as readers as they begin to journey toward reading leveled books.

Building Accuracy and Fluency

Accuracy and fluency are important aspects of reading, and are just as important as comprehension and decoding. Throughout the school year, no matter what unit you're teaching in reading workshop, you'll always touch on student's abilities to read with accuracy and fluency. And it's especially important to revisit the mini-lessons you teach in this unit throughout the grades as texts get more complex. These lessons will build upon on one another. As children begin to read just-right leveled texts in kindergarten, their books follow a pattern. These patterned texts contain a lot of sight words and a simple sentence structure. Many of your mini-lessons will zoom in on these patterns since they can be a tool to help children read accurately and fluently. Once students understand the pattern of a text, they can read each page more smoothly because they're not decoding each word. This marks the start of reading with phrasing.

As children read more difficult books, they sometimes begin to read in a much choppier voice. They no longer have a pattern to rely on. Therefore, they'll need to look more closely at punctuation marks to help them read, as well as think about the characters and mood of the story. They may begin to change their voices to reflect the voices of different characters in their books, which will also help them keep track of who is speaking.

We don't want children to forget that when we read, we gain information. It's very important to comprehend the meaning of the text. Therefore, some of your lessons for this unit should help children summarize or retell the text. Knowing what the book is about will help them accurately figure out unknown words, as well as make their voice match the mood of the story.

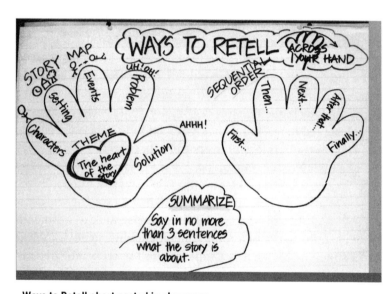

Ways to Retell chart posted in classroom

As always, keep on hand several read-alouds to help students develop the skills you are teaching. For instance, rhymes can help kindergarteners build their understanding of rhyming words. Make sure the nursery rhymes have picture clues to help students figure out which rhyme they're reading. Common songs and chants are also a good resource for building fluency, for example, "Who Stole the Cookies from the Cookie Jar?," "Teddy Bear, Teddy Bear," "Row, Row, Row Your Boat," "The Wheels on the Bus," "The ABC Song," and "Happy Birthday."

Some books that support fluent reading include *Please, Puppy, Please* and *Please, Baby, Please* by Spike Lee and Tony Lewis Lee, *Yo! Yes?* by Chris Raschka, *The Carrot Seed* by Ruth Kauss, and Mo Willems' Elephant and Piggie books, including *My Friend is Sad* and *I Am Invited to a Party*. These books encourage children to read in expressive and smooth voices, and their illustrations really help tell the story and make students enthusiastic about reading.

Reading poetry is also a great way to work on fluency and expression since poems have a natural rhythm and beat. Poems are especially good to use with second graders when you want a short text for practice work.

ELL Tip

Creating innovations on familiar texts can engage ELLs and provide opportunities for them to practice reading orally in a smooth voice. Some good choices are *Brown Bear, Brown Bear, What Do You See?* by Bill Martin, Jr. and Eric Carle, *Today Is Monday* by Eric Carle, *In a Dark, Dark Wood* by Christine Ross, *It Looked Like Spilt Milk* by Charles G. Shaw, and *I Went Walking* by Sue Williams. Children can create their own versions of these repetitive texts. You can also have them create their own miniature books around an upcoming holiday or a theme. For example, students may make a simple list book about getting ready for winter that follows the pattern, "In winter, I put on my . . ." This activity will also help them learn important vocabulary words.

Some poetry books that students love to read aloud include *Honey, I Love and Other Love Poems* by Eloise Greenfield, *Touch the Poem* by Arnold Adoff and Lisa Desimini, *Hopscotch Love: A Family Treasury of Love Poems* by Nikki Grimes, and *All the Small Poems and Fourteen More* by Valerie Worth.

Finally, you might also take short excerpts from chapter books and place them on the overhead. When you're looking for excerpts, choose sections with dialogue and a variety of punctuation marks.

In the conference note below, the teacher observes that Simon, a struggling first-grade reader, has basic sight word knowledge (B) and can recognize and read these words well, and these skills help him to read smoothly (D). He also understands that books usually have a pattern, and he tries to figure out that pattern (A). This enables Simon to phrase the words in the text. One area he can use support in is anticipating surprise endings in the pattern books he reads (C).

As the note indicates, the teacher's later work with Simon will include making sure he rereads the books in his book bag to build fluency (F). She plans to encourage Simon to do this by telling him that he's getting ready to read a book out loud to the class during share time. He'll see an important purpose for practicing reading.

As the conference note on page 45 indicates, Lilly is an advanced reader in her first-grade classroom. She can read almost any book that she is given due to her great knowledge of sight words, as well as her ability to use several decoding strategies at once (D). However, Lilly reads in a monotone voice with little emphasis on who is speaking or what is happening in the story, so the teacher jots down that Lilly needs help building her expression (E). He might give Lilly a reading phone so she can practice listening to herself reading, and ask her to create a different voice for each character in her book.

Additional skills that Lilly can work on include using punctuation marks (question marks, exclamation points, ellipses, and quotation marks) to strengthen her fluency and expression (C), and paying more attention to shifting moods and character feelings as she reads to help her voice sound more interesting (G).

One fun way to celebrate this unit is by having students record themselves reading a book in a smooth, interesting voice and placing these recordings along with the texts in the listening center for future use. ELLs in your classroom can later listen to these tapes to foster their fluency and expression.

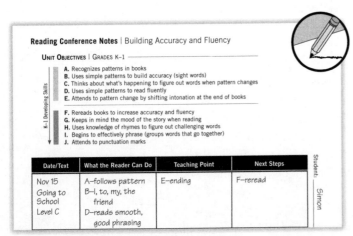

In this conference, the teacher works with Simon on changing his intonation at the end of the book.

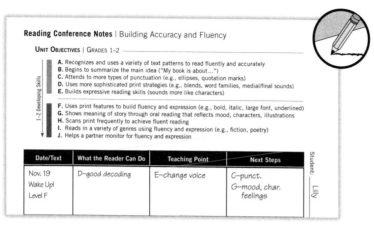

Reading Conference Notes | Building Accuracy and Fluency

UNIT OBJECTIVES | GRADES 1–2

A. Recognizes and uses a variety of text patterns to read fluently and accurately
B. Begins to summarize the main idea ("My book is about…")
C. Attends to more types of punctuation (e.g., ellipses, quotation marks)
D. Uses more sophisticated print strategies (e.g., blends, word families, medial/final sounds)
E. Builds expressive reading skills (sounds more like characters)

F. Uses print features to build fluency and expression (e.g., bold, italic, large font, underlined)
G. Shows meaning of story through oral reading that reflects mood, characters, illustrations
H. Scans print frequently to achieve fluent reading
I. Reads in a variety of genres using fluency and expression (e.g., fiction, poetry)
J. Helps a partner monitor for fluency and expression

Date/Text	What the Reader Can Do	Teaching Point	Next Steps
Nov. 19 Wake Up! Level F	D—good decoding	E—change voice	C—punct. G—mood, char. feelings

Student: Lilly

In future conferences with Lilly, her teacher will focus on objectives C and G.

Another celebration possibility is to ask children to read a text to their partner and then have their partners give a thumbs-up or thumbs-down based on how they sounded. You can encourage partners to practice giving each other specific compliments or suggestions for areas to work on.

Building Comprehension

The Building Comprehension unit is done at different points in the school year depending on which grade you teach. Kindergarteners read emergent storybooks early in the year to help them work toward leveled books. These "star" books help children build their story language, knowledge of story elements, and confidence to delve into reading. Students hear these books many times during the course of the school day. They feel comfortable with the texts during independent reading, and they begin to feel like they're readers. And since these books often have interesting plots, well-developed characters, and dialogue, they lend themselves to comprehension work. Additionally, emergent books usually are repetitive in plot and/or phrases and contain illustrations that help tell the story.

In the first and second grades, your focus might be on decoding skills earlier in the year, shifting to comprehension as the year progresses. Again, decide when this unit will work best for your class. Throughout it, you want students to begin to stop and think more about what's going on in the books they're reading. These books will include more developed characters that they can think about more deeply. If you haven't introduced the use of sticky notes to students to record their understanding of independent books, this is a good time to do so.

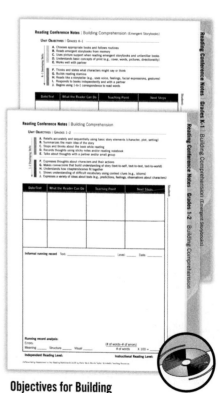

Objectives for Building Comprehension unit, Grades K–1 and 1–2
Print From CD/Copy From Appendix, pages 111 and 112

Early in the school year, we model how to stop and think about books during read-aloud time. We mark our read-alouds in advance with sticky notes that show our thinking. This activity helps students monitor their understanding of the books we read. It also shows them good places to stop and think, how to record their thinking using quick jots and symbols, and the kinds of thoughts they might have, which reinforces the good reading habits we want students to exhibit during independent reading. We encourage this thinking all year long during our carefully selected read-alouds. By doing this work regularly, the unit runs smoothly and with ease—and children immediately succeed in our mini-lessons.

Each page of the reading notebook is devoted to notes about a different book.

It's important to teach students how to use sticky notes and where to store them. If children have a reading notebook, they can write the title of the book on a page and stick all their notes below it when they are ready to read another book. You can also staple blank pages together to create a reader's log. Students can write each title of a book on a separate page and then glue the sticky notes below it. By second grade, they are often reading longer books with page numbers. Teach these older readers to write the page number on each note so they can refer to that page at a later date if they wish.

An abbreviation chart for sticky notes is an integral part of building your students' comprehension. The symbols on the chart allow students to record their thoughts quickly, and they can go back to reading their books. Post the chart in the classroom so they can look at it often to remind themselves of ways to rapidly jot down their thoughts. Children love using sticky notes and are proud of all the thoughts they record. They're eager to share their thoughts with their reading partners.

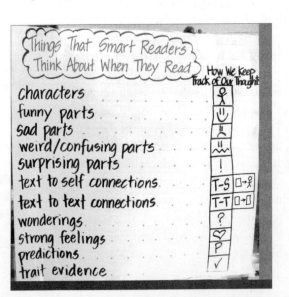

Post a chart of sticky-note abbreviations in the classroom as a reference for students.

Some emergent books for children to enjoy in this unit include *Are You My Mother?* By P.D. Eastman, *Caps for Sale* by Esphyr Slobodkina, *Corduroy* by Don Freeman, *Bark, George* by Jules Feiffer, *Do You Want to Be My Friend?* by Eric Carle, *The Gingerbread Man* by Karen Schmidt, and *Where the Wild Things Are* by Maurice Sendak.

Series that students are reading in your classroom can also become good read-alouds for this unit. These include Henry and Mudge by Cynthia Rylant, Frog and Toad by Arnold Lobel, Pinky and Rex by James Howe, Junie B. Jones by Barbara Park, and Amber Brown by Paula Danziger. Familiarity with the characters in a particular series helps build children's comprehension. You can also use any of your picture book read-alouds to work on comprehension strategies in this unit.

These simple puppets helped kindergarteners act out various texts.

One of the sample conference notes for this unit (page 48) focuses on Julisa, a kindergartener. Excited about reading a class favorite, *Bark, George*, Julisa knows where to sit and starts reading right away (A). After reading this book so often, she knows the story by heart (B), and her teacher observes her looking ahead to check the pictures to see which animal is inside George (C).

Julisa always wants her partner to read *Bark, George* first since she loves it so much. Her teacher decides to pull aside this partnership to teach the fairness of book choice (E). As a result, Julisa and her partner set up a schedule where they alternate choosing the book during partner time.

As the second sample shows, Sammy is reading level L books early in second grade. He usually has excellent comprehension and decoding skills. He's able to retell (A), and he stops and thinks throughout the book (C, D). In fact, Sammy has even begun to develop theories about Amelia (F)—he understands how foolish she is, which is at the heart of this series. However, as the books in the Amelia Bedelia series increase in difficulty, the vocabulary gets harder. Idioms, which Sammy is unfamiliar with, begin to appear. He tends to glance at them without trying to figure out what they mean (I). Expressions are a difficult skill to develop so Sammy's teacher plans to reteach this point over and over again.

ELL Tip

ELL students benefit from acting out stories or scenes from books. Through role playing, their comprehension grows. You may want to have students simply show you how they think the characters look at a particular moment in time or make gestures the characters might make. Students can build their repertoire of feeling words by stopping and showing different facial expressions the characters might have. This activity can also lend itself exploring how characters change since characters usually go through a range of emotions during the course of a book. Another option is to have pairs act out a page from a book. Select a page with two characters interacting. Each partner can invent what his or her character might say.

Also encourage all children to join in during your read-aloud so English language learners can be successful at reiterating the repetitive phrase they hear throughout the text, such as "Caps! Caps for Sale! 50 cents a cap!" from *Caps for Sale* by Esphyr Slobodkina.

English language learners who are shy about speaking may open up when they're allowed to create a puppet to hold and move around to act out a story. Keep these puppets alongside the accompanying books for use during center time.

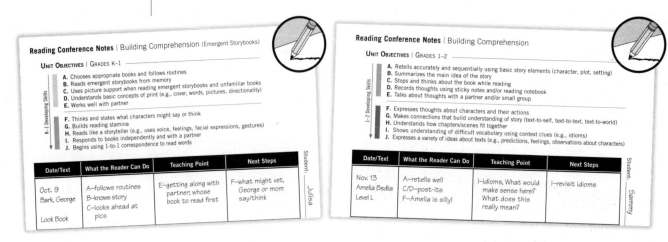

Reading Conference Notes | Building Comprehension (Emergent Storybooks)

UNIT OBJECTIVES | GRADES K–1

K–1 Developing Skills

A. Chooses appropriate books and follows routines
B. Reads emergent storybooks from memory
C. Uses picture support when reading emergent storybooks and unfamiliar books
D. Understands basic concepts of print (e.g., cover, words, pictures, directionality)
E. Works well with partner

F. Thinks and states what characters might say or think
G. Builds reading stamina
H. Reads like a storyteller (e.g., uses voice, feelings, facial expressions, gestures)
I. Responds to books independently and with a partner
J. Begins using 1-to-1 correspondence to read words

Date/Text	What the Reader Can Do	Teaching Point	Next Steps
Oct. 9 Bark, George Look Book	A–follows routines B–knows story C–looks ahead at pics	E–getting along with partner; whose book to read first	F–what might vet, George or mom say/think

Student: Julisa

Reading Conference Notes | Building Comprehension

UNIT OBJECTIVES | GRADES 1–2

1–2 Developing Skills

A. Retells accurately and sequentially using basic story elements (character, plot, setting)
B. Summarizes the main idea of the story
C. Stops and thinks about the book while reading
D. Records thoughts using sticky notes and/or reading notebook
E. Talks about thoughts with a partner and/or small group

F. Expresses thoughts about characters and their actions
G. Makes connections that build understanding of story (text-to-self, text-to-text, text-to-world)
H. Understands how chapters/scenes fit together
I. Understands difficult vocabulary using context clues (e.g., idioms)
J. Expresses a variety of ideas about texts (e.g., predictions, feelings, observations about characters)

Date/Text	What the Reader Can Do	Teaching Point	Next Steps
Nov. 13 Amelia Bedlia Level L	A–retells well C/D–post-its F–Amelia is silly!	I–idioms, What would make sense here? What does this really mean?	I–revisit idioms

Student: Sammy

In a future conference, the teacher will work with Julisa on thinking about expressing what one of the characters in *Bark, George* might say or do (F).

Teaching points that focus on difficult skills often have to be repeated in several conferences.

To celebrate your readers' growing understanding of the books they read, you may want to have each student create a poster display that includes sticky notes that show their thoughts and a book review. They can also talk about what they've written on their sticky notes with a partner or the whole class.

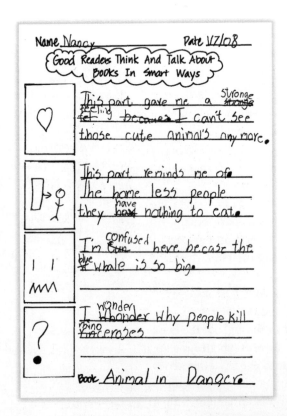

Nancy's poster reveals her feelings about the book, the connections she makes, and questions she has about it.

Partners can also decide on a book to act out. They can create puppets and perform for the class. To prompt them, you can serve as narrator and turn the pages of the book. Invite another class on the grade that knows the books your students are presenting.

Karin's | Classroom Notes

Children get very excited when they receive a new reading tool. Sometimes this excitement translates into the overuse of that tool. This often happens in my classroom with sticky notes. Throughout the years, I've noticed that children compete with each other to see who can use the most sticky notes in a day. Because this distracts them from their comprehension work, I now limit how many sticky notes each student receives for each reading workshop. I give out two or three sticky notes per book during the unit. At the end, as a part of our celebration, each child gets his or her own pack of sticky notes. This is very exciting for them! They've graduated to choosing how many sticky notes they need for a book! By this time, they've learned how many sticky notes they really need, and I no longer have to monitor their use.

Building Your Book Talk

Once students are using comprehension skills with confidence, they are better able to talk with partners or in small groups about the books they're reading. This unit gives them the conversational tools to help them master book talk. They learn conversation prompts as well as how to use a partner effectively to build their comprehension of the text.

Students may begin by reacting to the book through laughter, and then work toward staying on topic and developing and supporting theories. They extend their conversations by using the word *because* and may begin to dispute each other's ideas. In this unit, kindergarteners and first graders work with reading partners, whereas some second-grade classrooms may move students into small book clubs—a group of four or five who read and discuss a particular book or series. These groups plan what to read in advance and are ready to discuss the book during book club time. The members often "talk off of" their sticky notes and build upon one another's ideas.

Some great series for the book talk unit are Poppleton by Mark Teague, Arthur by Lillian Hoban, and A–Z Mysteries by Ron Roy. Good picture books to use include *When Sophie Gets*

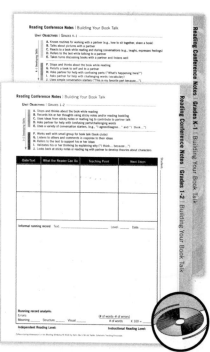

Objectives for Building Your Book Talk Unit, Grades K–1 and 1–2
Print From CD/Copy From Appendix, pages 113 and 114

Angry . . . Really, Really Angry by Molly Bang, *The Recess Queen* by Alexis O'Neill and Laura Huliska-Beith, *King of the Playground* by Phyllis Reynolds Naylor, *Enemy Pie* by Derek Munson, *The Other Dog* by Madeline L'Engle, and *Dirty Bertie* by David Roberts. The characters and plots intrigue students, they often relate to the events in the stories. Their interest and connection encourages them to talk with partners during read-aloud time, so this is an important time to model how to stop and talk to partners. Children benefit from practicing this work during class read-alouds, and this skill transfers to partnership reading time.

As the sample conference notes indicate, first grader Caroline is engaged in the book she's reading. She reacts appropriately to the text (C) and uses sticky notes to record her thinking (F). Although Caroline stays on topic (D), she fails to respond to what her partner says (E).

Her teacher chooses to work on extending book talk by having her listen to her partner and respond "I agree/disagree . . . because . . ." This prompt will keep the book talk more focused.

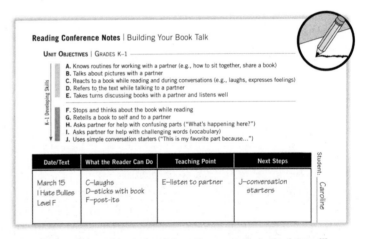

Caroline's teacher plans to teach her other prompts in the future (J).

Lawrence is a successful second-grade reader who has good comprehension. This is displayed by his ability to stop and think during reading (A), record his thinking (B), talk off of his sticky notes (C), and use a variety of conversation starters (E).

However, Lawrence's teacher thinks his conversations could grow if he used the text more to support his thinking (H). She decides to teach Lawrence to open the book to a scene that supports his idea during book talk and show it to his book club.

Throughout the unit, children are working on their book talk. At the end of the unit, you can celebrate their progress by having partnerships discuss their favorite books. You may also want to have the

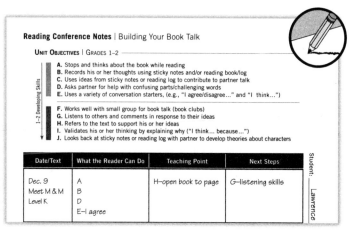

Reading Conference Notes | Building Your Book Talk

UNIT OBJECTIVES | GRADES 1–2

1–2 Developing Skills

A. Stops and thinks about the book while reading
B. Records his or her thoughts using sticky notes and/or reading book/log
C. Uses ideas from sticky notes or reading log to contribute to partner talk
D. Asks partner for help with confusing parts/challenging words
E. Uses a variety of conversation starters, (e.g., "I agree/disagree..." and "I think...")

F. Works well with small group for book talk (book clubs)
G. Listens to others and comments in response to their ideas
H. Refers to the text to support his or her ideas
I. Validates his or her thinking by explaining why ("I think... because...")
J. Looks back at sticky notes or reading log with partner to develop theories about characters

Date/Text	What the Reader Can Do	Teaching Point	Next Steps
Dec. 9 Meet M & M Level K	A B D E—I agree	H—open book to page	G—listening skills

Student: Lawrence

In the future, Lawrence's teacher may work to build his listening skills so his talk grows even more (G).

whole class join in a book talk about a favorite class read-aloud; talking with a larger group of children is more difficult and should be celebrated. Encourage students to keep a tally of how many conversational prompts they use during this class discussion. Like any real book club, you can end the celebration with a special snack, such as cheese and crackers and sparkling apple cider.

As part of the celebration, have students share their Book Club Logs with the whole class. They can even discuss whether the class should read the book they studied in their book club.

Book Club Log

Book Club Name: Book club with friends
Members: Manny, Alex, Marurambi, Kathy, Boryd, Haley

Date	What We Worked On	Assignment Box
1/17/06		Poppleton and Henry and mudge
1/17/06	They say nice words	We will finish our book
1/18/06	we worked on people shareing.	We will swich books. and read 4c
1/19/06	We worked on pushing the Quire voses	We are going to Read the next two chapters
1/20/06	We worked on adding on ideas	Read the rest at home.
1/21/06	sticking to one idea at a time.	Read the rest of the book.

Book Club Log

Book Club Name: The amazing friendship Studyers
Members: Jessica and Ashley

Date	What We Worked On	Assignment Box
1/17/06		Arthur's first sleepover half of the Book
1/17/06	We talked about what friends do and how they Care about eachother	Add more postits and read more of the book to see what else friends do
1/18/06	how friends treat eachother	Junie B. Jones and A little monkey Business 2 chapters
1/19/06	What kind of person they are	Junie B. Jones and A little monkey Business 3,4
1/20/06	how friendship Changes	Junie B. Jones and a little monkey Business 5,6
1/23/06	HoW friends solve problems	Junie B. Jones and a little monkey Busniess 7,8

These students kept track of their discussion points and the skills they were working on in Book Club Logs.

Objectives for Nonfiction Reading Grades K–1 and 1–2
Print From CD/Copy From Appendix, pages 115 and 116

Nonfiction Reading Strategies

All year long, students read in a variety of genres; however, this unit focuses their attention on nonfiction. So far, students have focused mainly on strategies involved in reading fiction, but reading nonfiction is very different from reading fiction. In order to be successful with this unit, students will need to change how they read. They'll need to know how the structure of nonfiction books differs from fiction. To introduce the nonfiction structure to students, you can show the table of contents and index and point out headings, photos, diagrams, and other text features as you read certain sections, or you may read the books cover to cover. They'll need to learn how to use these features to gain information from their books.

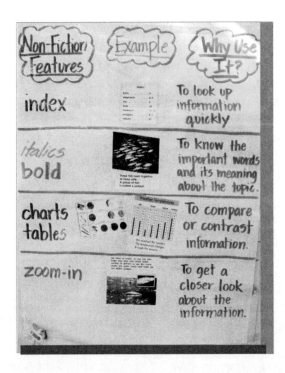

Charts can be a valuable tool to support students in the Nonfiction Reading Strategies unit.

Children are often very excited about starting to read a new genre. They look forward to learning about a topic and gathering information that interests them. There are wonderful authors whose nonfiction appeals to young readers. Gail Gibbons' books have a variety of nonfiction features and topics that interest children. Simon Seymour also writes many excellent nonfiction books for more advanced readers. Look through your leveled library as well for simple nonfiction texts to read to your class. Children's educational magazines, such as Scholastic's *Let's Find Out* and *Time Magazine's Time for Kids*, offer many nonfiction articles that often come with a poster-size copy for the teacher to use during shared reading as well as a standard-size reproducible page. After doing some whole class work, you can give each student his or her own copy for continued practice.

In this sample conference note, Rosa, a kindergartener, has chosen a book about animals, *Black and White* by Dorothy Avery. She has a lot of prior knowledge about animals (B) because of all the nonfiction animal books she's looked at this year. When the teacher listens to Rosa discuss the book, he notices that Rosa zooms in on one page about dogs (D), rather than accumulating information from all the pages of the book and sharing that information. The teacher decides to introduce taking a picture walk prior to reading (C) during Rosa's next conference so she'll have a better understanding of what the whole book is about first.

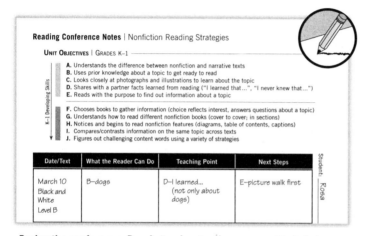

Reading Conference Notes | Nonfiction Reading Strategies

UNIT OBJECTIVES | GRADES K–1

K–1 Developing Skills

A. Understands the difference between nonfiction and narrative texts
B. Uses prior knowledge about a topic to get ready to read
C. Looks closely at photographs and illustrations to learn about the topic
D. Shares with a partner facts learned from reading ("I learned that...", "I never knew that...")
E. Reads with the purpose to find out information about a topic

F. Chooses books to gather information (choice reflects interest, answers questions about a topic)
G. Understands how to read different nonfiction books (cover to cover; in sections)
H. Notices and begins to read nonfiction features (diagrams, table of contents, captions)
I. Compares/contrasts information on the same topic across texts
J. Figures out challenging content words using a variety of strategies

Date/Text	What the Reader Can Do	Teaching Point	Next Steps	Student: Rosa
March 10 Black and White Level B	B–dogs	D–I learned... (not only about dogs)	E–picture walk first	

During the conference, Rosa's teacher teaches a prompt to help her focus on other aspects of the book.

Kirin's first-grade teacher has frequently observed her reading books outside of reading workshop. Kirin has well-developed comprehension skills so the teacher decides to use the Grades 1–2 conference sheet with her (see page 54). As the sample conference note shows, Kirin is reading *Balcony Garden* by Rebecca Weber. By looking at the photographs (B) she understands that the book is an example of a how-to (A).

Kirin reads the book from cover to cover, much like a narrative text. She pays little attention to its table of contents, so the teacher concentrates on showing her how to use the table of contents to help her read the text (D).

In the future, Kirin's teacher may want to work on helping her accumulate the text by using prompts, such as, "This book is all about . . . For example, ..."(E).

There are many ways to celebrate nonfiction reading. During this unit, children begin to realize how much they can learn from reading nonfiction books. They love to share their new information with their friends, and it's important to give them the opportunity to teach others all their newfound facts. One simple way to do this

ELL Tip

During your nonfiction study, the whole class will probably need to move back a level since nonfiction reading poses many vocabulary challenges. Your English language learners may need to move back even farther if they have a very limited vocabulary. Choose books around a concept these students are familiar with. Revisit some social studies or science topics that they've learned this year, such as weather, family, school, community helpers, plants, or animals. Although the rest of the class may have more of a choice in their reading materials, it's important to guide ELL students to books they can read successfully. You may wish to create a nonfiction reading center for these children by compiling book bags around these familiar concepts. They can choose a book bag containing a topic they're interested in, and, since you put the bags together, you still have control over the reading materials. Be sure these books contain vivid photographs so children can gain information from them. The books can be of varying levels because students will pull out most of the facts from the photographs.

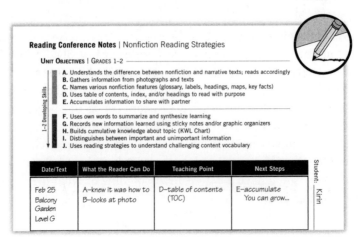

A. Understands the difference between nonfiction and narrative texts; reads accordingly
B. Gathers information from photographs and texts
C. Names various nonfiction features (glossary, labels, headings, maps, key facts)
D. Uses table of contents, index, and/or headings to read with purpose
E. Accumulates information to share with partner

F. Uses own words to summarize and synthesize learning
G. Records new information learned using sticky notes and/or graphic organizers
H. Builds cumulative knowledge about topic (KWL Chart)
I. Distinguishes between important and unimportant information
J. Uses reading strategies to understand challenging content vocabulary

Date/Text	What the Reader Can Do	Teaching Point	Next Steps
Feb 25 Balcony Garden Level G	A–knew it was how to B–looks at photo	D–table of contents (TOC)	E–accumulate You can grow...

Student: Kirin

In the conference, Kirin remembers writing how-to's in kindergarten and expresses this to her teacher.

is to provide different paper choices that children are familiar with from their nonfiction writing. Each paper choice represents a different nonfiction feature like zoom ins, maps, diagrams, or charts. Allow students to select one feature to show others. If they were reading in centers around a topic, you can collate all the features together to create an All About book. Otherwise, you can display the features separately, as the samples show, on a bulletin board after students have had an opportunity to share them.

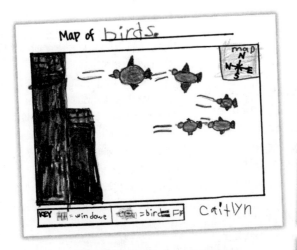

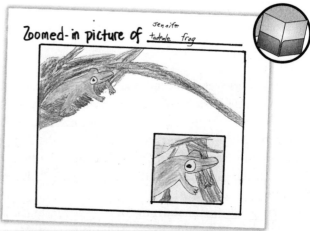

These students used the following nonfiction paper choices: map, zoom in, and chart.

Another celebration option is to have groups work together to create a magazine. Children should be familiar with the style, format, and features of magazines. Mondo's *Safari* magazines, which are differentiated by reading level and grade level, are wonderful for students to read and replicate. Students can work together to create their own issue and include it in the class library *Safari* basket. (Be sure to laminate the magazine before adding it to the library.)

Cover   page 17   page 18

Second-grade students who studied the rainforest created this issue. In one feature, Jay created his own play, which was entertaining and informative.

Character Investigation

As the year progresses, students will have honed their decoding skills. This can create a situation in which some children begin to lag behind in their comprehension skills. It's important to remind these students that we read for enjoyment and meaning—books provide windows into new worlds and adventures.

Books centered around a particular character help young readers build their comprehension skills. They become familiar with this character and the author's writing style. They have come to know these characters, and this familiarity helps strengthen their envisioning skills: They can envision what they look like, where they live, and who their friends are. Students are also able to become more accurate in their predictions of what will happen in their story based on the knowledge they have of the characters. Their predictions become more tied to the text, and they use accompanying text evidence.

The characters in their books come to life and become "friends." Children make more connections to these characters and their own lives, as well as to

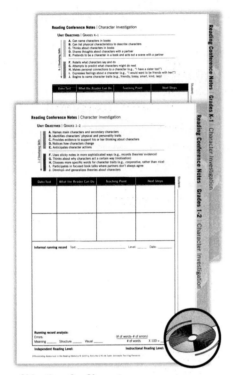

Objectives for Character Investigation Unit, Grades K–1 and 1–2
Print From CD/Copy From Appendix, pages 117 and 118

other books they've read with similar characters. You'll frequently hear them saying, "Oh, he's just like . . . "

As students build these comprehension skills, they'll begin to learn character traits based on actions and dialogue. Most children start out with words, like *nice* and *bad* to describe characters. We want to move them toward more specific vocabulary words, like *friendly*, *bossy*, *smart*, and *lazy*. Support students in making more descriptive words part of their language by creating a class chart based on the vocabulary from your read-alouds. Model using these new vocabulary words during your read-alouds, and allow time for students to practice using the words during read-aloud book talk.

Good readers think about what the characters are like in books

Book	Character	Character Trait
Tom's Trousers	Mom	thoughtful
Playing with Dad	Dad	playful
The Toytown Helicopter	Tow Truck	considerate
Sledding	Dad	clumsy
I Am Invited to a Party!	Piggie	silly
The Snowy Day	Peter	adventurous
The Recess Queen	Jean	mean, bossy
David Goes To School	David	trouble-maker naughty
Carlo Likes Reading	Carlos	smart, clever
Dirty Bertie	Bertie	disgusting, gross

Character Traits chart posted in classroom.

Some great read-alouds that support this unit include *The Recess Queen* by Alexis O'Neill, the Mr. and Mrs. Green series by Keith Baker, the Willy series by Anthony Browne, *Rosie and Michael* by Judith Viorst, *Dirty Bertie* by David Roberts, and any of the Brand New Readers. These Brand New Readers books are usually levels B–D, and students enjoy reading them. Each four-book pack is centered around the same character, so students accumulate information about the character. These mentor texts give children the opportunity to try out some of the same reading work we want them to do independently. Your read-aloud time more closely resembles independent reading because you're using simple books to model the thinking work you want them to do.

In preparing this sample conference note, the teacher observes Deondre, a typical kindergarten reader, reading level C books loudly at his reading spot. He is able to tell the teacher who the characters are (A) and use descriptive words like *little* and *fat* (B). She decides to extend Deondre's reading work to include thinking about the characters and what they do (C).

Kai Ling, a gifted second grader, is already reading level N books, like the Judy Moody series. She is able to identify all the characters in her books, as well as keep track of them (A). She envisions well when reading and can describe the character's traits (B). She is a very verbal student, and uses a lot of difficult vocabulary when talking about a character's traits and giving evidence to support those traits (C).

The teacher would like her to translate her verbal skills to written words. This will help Kai Ling document her thinking and remember it more for book club work. In the conference, the teacher introduces how to jot thoughts on sticky notes (F).

You can be very creative with your celebrations during the Character Investigation unit of study. For example, lead a character parade around the school. Have children dress up like the character they studied and visit different classrooms. See if other students can guess who they are. Be sure to call students by their character names all day long.

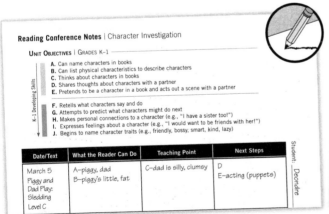

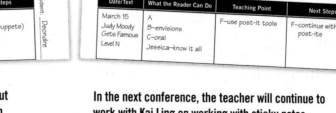

The next steps might involve using puppets to act out scenes in the books with a partner (E). This will help Deondre talk about the characters with his partner (D).

In the next conference, the teacher will continue to work with Kai Ling on working with sticky notes.

Nicolette is dressed up as Nate the Great, with her buddy Sludge.

First graders Zachary and Isaac become Henry and Mudge. The teacher, dressed as Willy from Anthony Browne's series, introduces them to the audience.

Or create your own Character Theater in your classroom, and challenge students to act out a scene from their books with partners. Students can make props and perform a scene for parents, friends, and classmates. Encourage them to create posters to decorate the room and show the different characters they love. Parents can help with this activity by working on the props and costumes.

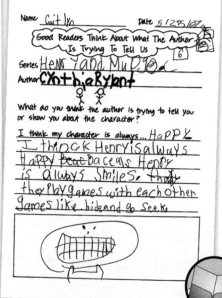

This example shows first grader Eric identifying the problem and the solution.

First grader Raymond made important connections between himself and *Fox in Love*.

We always hope that our readers are able to grasp the message that the author is conveying about the characters he or she has created in a series. First grader Caitlyn uses a character trait to describe Henry. Note that she includes text evidence for support.

And throughout the unit, students can celebrate their thinking with different responses to literature. Allow students to show problems characters face in different books since they'll be reading many books featuring the character. This will build their ability to accumulate information about their character across texts and series.

Response sheets can also help children make connections between the text and their own lives. Including a prompt that you want students to use during book talk, like "This part reminds me of when . . ." helps them take ownership of this language and reinforces its use. Over time, children begin to go beyond simple connections and focus on deeper ones that help them understand the story.

Reading Centers

Reading centers is an enjoyable unit to do at different points during the year. It breaks up the routines for reading workshop and allows children to work together to study a specific topic. In kindergarten and some first grades, reading centers can take the form of a concept study. Children can learn about different concepts, such as the alphabet, numbers, shapes, and colors, by gathering information about the concept and developing important ideas about it. They know how to read concept books and can anticipate what letter, number, shape, or color might be on the next page. Additionally, children can compare and contrast books in their reading centers and share this information with reading partners.

We like to use the following concept books in this unit: Tana Hoban math books, *ABC T-Rex* by Bernard Most, *Eating the Alphabet: Fruits and Vegetable from A–Z* by Lois Ehlert, *Alphabet City* by Stephen T. Johnson, *Dr. Seuss' ABC: An Amazing Alphabet Book* by Dr. Seuss, *The Icky Bug Counting Book* by Jerry Pallotta, *Anno's Counting Book* by Mitsumasa Anno, *Roar! A Noisy Counting Book* by Pamela Dunkin Edwards, *Color Zoo* by Lois Ehlert, *White Rabbit's Color Book* by Allen Baker, *Growing Colors* by Bruce McMillan, *Mouse Shapes* by Ellen Stoll Walsh, and *The Shape of Things* by Dayle Ann Dodds.

For second graders, and some first graders, it's more appropriate to have reading centers constructed around a series or a concept like friendship, family, or school. Children can build upon the skills they mastered in the previous unit on character investigation. They'll get to know a particular series, or a set of friends in one book, and begin to develop theories about these characters. Their book talk will increase dramatically. As they read longer books that have more chapters, students need to work on accumulating ideas and information about the texts. Getting to know a series well helps them accomplish this. They can anticipate how the text will unfold and become familiar with the author's writing style.

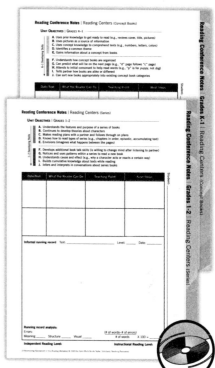

Objectives for Reading Centers Unit, Grades K–1 and 1–2
Print From CD/Copy From Appendix, pages 119 and 120

The study of concept books helps kindergarten ELLs tremendously. Concept books offer a lot of vivid picture support, which helps these students tackle the text.

They are able to learn important vocabulary and review basic concepts that they need. Choose simple books that have the same format for these students to look at. For example, display several alphabet books where each page has a letter and a picture of one thing that begins with that letter. This gives children practice in naming the letter, number, shape, or color. Later on in the unit, they can add the object name, like *one apple*, *red apple*, *round apple*, or *a is for apple*. You can also have ELL students read picture cards around the concept. Make up your own cards with a picture to match the concept and a concept word. Laminate and place the cards in a plastic bag for students to read independently.

Support your older English language learners by encouraging them to read the same series you're modeling during whole class instruction. Because these students are more familiar with the series, they're able to apply your expressive interpretation to their own reading. Choose series that don't have too many secondary characters, setting changes, or complex plots.

Some great series include Biscuit by Alyssa Satin Capucilli, Baby Bear from Rigby, Max and Ruby by Rosemary Wells, Mr. Putter and Tabby by Cynthia Rylant, Iris and Walter by Elissa Guest, Little Bear by E. Homelund Minarik, Poppleton by Cynthia Rylant, Henry and Mudge by Cynthia Rylant, Frog and Toad by Arnold Lobel, Fluffy by Kate McMullan, Minnie and Moo by Denys Cazet, Pinky and Rex by James Howe, Horrible Harry by Suzy Kline, Junie B. Jones by Barbara Park, and Julian by Ann Cameron. Any series that you have multiple copies of in your classroom will work for this unit. Most series relate to friendship, school, and/or family so it's easy to make the unit concept more specific.

The sample conference note below focuses on Shana, a kindergartener who comes to school with knowledge of about half the alphabet. To build her alphabet recognition skills, she is studying the concept of letters. Her teacher has read *Chicka Chicka Boom Boom* by Bill Martin Jr. and John Archambault to the class many times before (A). Shana understands that the topic is the alphabet (D). In the conference, the teacher has Shana sing the ABC song to herself to help her figure out the next letter in the alphabet (C). A good follow-up to this conference might be to have Shana try out this strategy in other alphabet books where the letters look different (F).

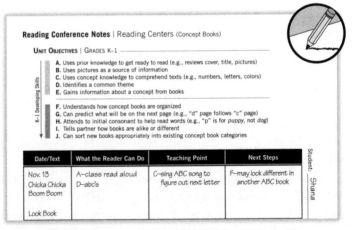

Shana knows the ABC song, so she can use it to help her identify unknown letters.

The next sample conference note (page 61) focuses on Dillon, a first grader who knows a lot about Clifford the big red dog. He's seen Clifford on TV. He understands how the Clifford series proceeds, and he knows it's the kind of book he needs to read from beginning to end (D). As the note shows, Dillon is also able to imagine what happens in the story and can make strong pictures in his mind (E).

However, the teacher notices that Dillon and his partner are not reading books in the same series, which makes it difficult to talk about the books together and develop theories. In the conference, she teaches Dillon how to make a plan with a partner to read a book from the same series (C). In the future, she'll work on furthering their partner plans by having them decide what to talk about in advance (C).

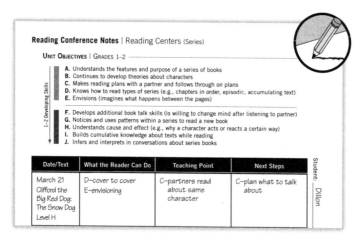

Reading Conference Notes | Reading Centers (Series)

Unit Objectives | **Grades 1–2**

1–2 Developing Skills

A. Understands the features and purpose of a series of books
B. Continues to develop theories about characters
C. Makes reading plans with a partner and follows through on plans
D. Knows how to read types of series (e.g., chapters in order, episodic, accumulating text)
E. Envisions (imagines what happens between the pages)

F. Develops additional book talk skills (is willing to change mind after listening to partner)
G. Notices and uses patterns within a series to read a new book
H. Understands cause and effect (e.g., why a character acts or reacts a certain way)
I. Builds cumulative knowledge about texts while reading
J. Infers and interprets in conversations about series books

Date/Text	What the Reader Can Do	Teaching Point	Next Steps
March 21 Clifford the Big Red Dog: The Snow Dog Level H	D–cover to cover E–envisioning	C–partners read about same character	C–plan what to talk about

Student: Dillon

Planning ahead will give Dillon and his partner the opportunity to look for evidence to support their thinking before they meet for talk time.

A great way to celebrate students' knowledge of concept books is to have them create their own concept book. This task also helps you assess their knowledge of letters, numbers, colors, and shapes.

| Cover | page 1 | Cover | page 6 |

Kindergarteners created these concept books. They chose a theme and related the concept to that theme.

Older students can create a new book based on the series they read. These young writers can think about the characters they need to include, problems the characters might face, solutions they might try, the setting, the language the mentor author uses and his or her style, and the layout of the text. They write these books with the knowledge that the character remains the same throughout the series.

This gifted first grader was very successful in writing his own book based on the A–Z Mysteries series.

Cover

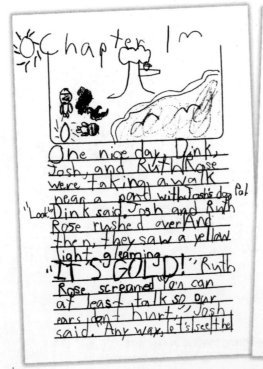

page 1   **page 7**

Another celebration possibility is to have partners work together to produce a magazine article based on their theme.

These gifted first graders had been reading *Time for Kids* all year long so they were familiar with its format and style. The paper choice supported their work in creating their own issue about friendship. They devised theories and provide support for them in the article.

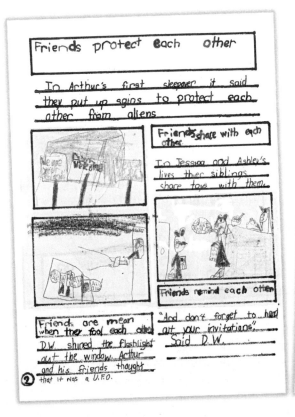

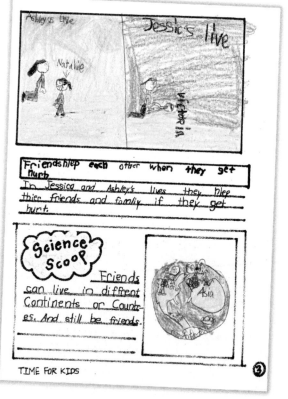

A fun idea is to have students create a board game based on the series they read. This group of first graders used their knowledge of the Little Bill series by Bill Cosby to produce this game. In addition to showing their understanding of the series and its characters, the game cards help test each other's knowledge.

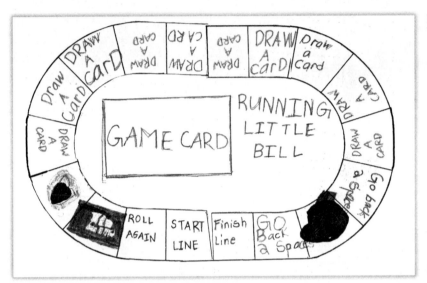

Students even paid attention to details in the pictures they drew on their Little Bill game cards

Objectives for Shared Reading Texts Unit, Grades K–1
Print From CD/Copy From Appendix, page 121

Shared Reading Texts

This unit helps early readers build their confidence before entering the world of just-right books. It serves as a stepping stone from emergent storybooks to leveled books and allows children to begin one-to-one correspondence in familiar books. Their reading stamina continues to grow. They remember the text of songs, poems, and small copies of big books from hearing them so many times during shared reading, and this knowledge helps them move from familiar texts to unfamiliar texts with greater ease. Children's fluency and expression grow as well because they're learning more sight words and starting to build a knowledge of early print strategies.

For this unit, be sure to use any texts that students are familiar with and can read well. Basic songs such as the "Happy Birthday" song and the "Alphabet" song are great additions to students' book bags.

The kindergarten teacher who wrote the sample conference note on page 65 knows that her student Jobin has a collection of poems and songs for this unit of study. He knows the routines of reading workshop, and he goes to his reading spot right away (A). He reads and sings the whole time (B) and remembers the songs well (D).

Jobin's teacher would like him to use the picture cues in the poems and songs to help him figure out the title of the songs and poems on each page (C). Sometimes Jobin sings a song that isn't on the page he's looking at and the picture support would help him focus.

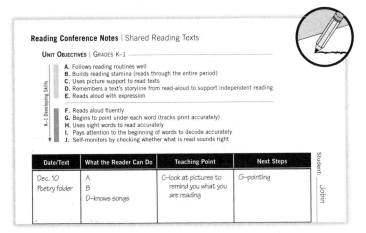

In the future, Jobin's teacher will work with him on pointing at the words on each page (G).

Celebrate the end of this unit with a musical. Individual children can choose a favorite song to sing in front of the class while the audience sings along. Another option is for students to think of movements to match the text in a poem and perform it for the class. Children enjoy being creative with these movements, and the whole audience is engaged.

Closely observing students as they read gives you a lot of insight to use during assessment. The individualized Reading Conference Notes sheets, although brief, provide a window into what each student is capable of as well as where to go next in your instruction. The range of objectives for each unit allows you to differentiate to meet the needs of all the readers in your class.

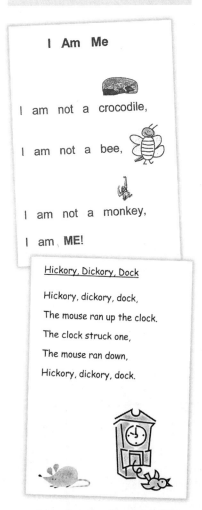

Some favorite classroom songs

Chapter 4

Conferring to Reach Readers at All Levels

"When we listen to kids, ask them questions, and watch them closely, we learn not only what they understand but also what they don't understand."

STEPHANIE HARVEY AND ANNE GOUDVIS, (2007) *STRATEGIES THAT WORK*

As a new school year begins, you can expect to welcome students of all abilities into your classroom—children who are going to perform at grade level, children who need extra support, and children who have a good grasp of the content and need an additional challenge. In order to reach the range of abilities in your classroom, this chapter describes students at each grade level (K–2) throughout the year.

In this chapter you will find answers to the following questions:

- What kinds of observations about students' reading can I make?
- How do I analyze and prioritize the objectives?
- How can I differentiate assessment and instruction to help support all the readers in my classroom?
- How will the readers in my classroom grow as they advance through the primary grades?
- How can different conversations go as I confer with many levels of readers in my classroom?

Portrait of Readers Early in the Year

Early in the school year, the focus in the reading workshop is on routines regardless of which grade you teach. Even children who have participated in reading workshops in previous grades need a refresher on expectations and the use of materials. And, because every classroom is unique and has its own management system, it's crucial to take the time to practice these routines early so your readers will have a successful year.

Supporting Kindergarten Readers at the Beginning of the School Year

Children start kindergarten with various levels of readiness. Some may have gone to preschools that are academic in nature, others may have attended preschools where the emphasis was on play, and many others may not have had any formal schooling. Beginning kindergarteners have been exposed to books in varying degrees, so you cannot assume that all your students are living "literate" lives. In the kindergarten classroom, you'll encounter children with a range of skills—from students who know the whole alphabet and may even be reading books, to those who have never held a book before and aren't sure how to turn the pages.

Therefore, it's best to start off the year by having children read from tabletop baskets that contain books in a wide range of levels, including fairy tales, folk tales, and books by popular authors like Eric Carle and Dr. Seuss, as well as familiar songs and rhymes.

Kindergarteners will soon learn how to read emergent storybooks and tell a story by looking at the pictures and using their imagination. They'll practice many readiness skills, such as how to handle books, turn pages, and where to begin reading and where to go next. Book shopping will play an important role in the reading workshop. Your early conferences will focus on many of the rules you've established in your classroom.

Ronny begins kindergarten with an understanding of how books are handled, and he holds the book right side up and turns the pages to follow the text. His text choices include books that he's familiar with and excited about. As Ronny reads *Brown Bear, Brown Bear, What Do You See?* by Bill Martin, Jr. and Eric Carle, the teacher observes that Ronny is able to tell the story through pictures in the book, and he eagerly recites the animals he sees on each page.

Based on these observations and the objectives of the first unit, Launching the Reading Workshop, Ronny's teacher might choose to work on one of the following:

- Understanding the routines of the reading workshop, which include reading with a quieter voice
- Reading independently first and then turning for partner reading time

Here's how a conference between Ronny and his teacher focusing on the teaching point of reading in a quieter voice:

Ms. B: That was great reading, Ronny! I love how you checked the pictures when you forgot which animal was coming up on the next page.

Ronny: Yeah, see, here's a duck.

Ms. B: I'm glad you're so excited about reading. When we're reading, we want to try to use a quieter voice, so other students can enjoy their books too. I call it using a one-inch voice.

(Ms. B shows a space of 1 inch with her fingers.)

Ms. B: Listen to how I read this part of your book with my one-inch voice.

(Ms. B reads enthusiastically, but quietly.)

Ronny: Oh.

Ms. B: Okay. Now you try reading with your one-inch voice.

(Ronny begins to read in a quieter voice, but he gets louder again. When Ms. B makes the 1-inch sign with her fingers, Ronny lowers his voice.)

Ms. B: That was much better. So if you forget again, you may see me make my one-inch sign, and you'll know to quiet down.

Ronny: Okay. I'm going to read this book again!

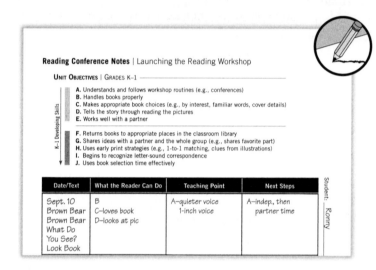

Ms. B recognizes Ronny's strengths and notes that he will need to continue to work on the routines of reading workshop, especially understanding that independent reading is later followed by partner reading.

SUPPORTING FIRST-GRADE READERS AT THE BEGINNING OF THE SCHOOL YEAR

At the start of first grade, children should be beginning readers. Most students have been exposed to just-right books and are reading books at Fountas and Pinnell levels B–D. These books have simple patterns, few sentences, recognizable sight words, and abundant picture support. Students reading at levels B–D have some basic sight word recognition, usually demonstrate 1-to-1 correspondence, know how to handle books, and are beginning to retell some events in stories.

It's crucial to assess students' reading levels early in the year because you may have readers who are ready for harder books or those who need extra support to read books that most of the children in your class are ready to tackle independently.

Destiny reads at level C, which is on-grade level for the beginning of the school year, so her teacher uses the Grade 1–2 Reading Conference Notes sheet. He notes that Destiny knows the routines of reading workshop including choosing books at her reading level and handling books properly. She's also able to tell the story using the pictures and some words. Based on these observations and the objectives for Launching the Reading Workshop, Destiny's teacher might choose to work on the following:

- Using early print strategies like matching the words to the pictures
- Using other early print strategies like looking at the initial letter of an unfamiliar word

Here's how a conference between Destiny and her teacher focusing on the first teaching point of matching words to pictures:

> **Mr. L:** Destiny, what are you reading today?

(Destiny displays *A Day at School*.)

> **Mr. L:** Oh, *A Day at School!* I bet you know a lot about that, since you go to school!

> **Destiny:** Uh-huh.

> **Mr. L:** You know, I was watching you when I sent everyone back to their spots to read, and I noticed how you quickly took out your book bag and got started reading right away. I'm so proud of you! You remember just what to do when it's time for reading workshop.

> **Destiny:** Yes.

> **Mr. L:** Can you tell me a little about the book?

(Destiny begins to turn the pages and tell a few things that happen in the story.)

> **Mr. L:** Let's read a little bit. What page are you up to in this book?

> **Destiny:** Right here!

(Destiny reads page 5 and says "cards" for "math." On his Reading Conference Notes, Mr. L jots down that he'd like her to pay closer attention to the pictures and make sure the words match the pictures.)

> **Mr. L:** Destiny, I'd like you to stop reading right here. Good readers look closely at the pictures to help them with the words. Let me show you what I mean.

(Mr. L looks at the previous page that shows the illustration of a student who has a book beside her and is writing. He intentionally misreads this page so he can model self-correction for Destiny.)

> **Mr. L:** Let me read this part to you: "I like to read books." Oh, wait a minute. The girl has a pencil in her hand. Let me read it again: "I like to write stories." That's better. That matches the picture. Now look more closely at this picture and then read the page again.

(Destiny correctly reads the words, "I like to do math.")

> **Mr. L:** Great job! What did you see in the picture?

> **Destiny:** The cards have numbers!

> **Mr. L:** That's right, so make sure to look at all the pictures closely when you're reading.

Reading Conference Notes | Launching the Reading Workshop

UNIT OBJECTIVES | GRADES 1–2

1–2 Developing Skills

A. Understands and follows workshop routines (e.g., book choice, book handling, conferences)
B. Tells the story through reading the pictures and some words
C. Is developing good book talk skills (e.g., faces the speaker, takes turns)
D. Uses early print strategies (e.g., 1-to-1 matching, picture clues, letter-sound correspondence)
E. Chooses appropriate independent reading books

F. Builds reading stamina (reads through the entire period)
G. Identifies basic story elements (plot, characters, setting)
H. Begins to retell in sequential order using story elements
I. Shows evidence of comprehension through thoughtful predictions
J. Envisions parts of the story well (can see what is happening without the support of illustrations)

Date/Text	What the Reader Can Do	Teaching Point	Next Steps
Sept. 12 A Day at School Level C	A—knows routines B	D—match words to pics	D—more print work

Student: Destiny

Mr. L understands that early print strategies will elevate Destiny's ability to read independently. This is an objective Mr. L knows will take time to nurture.

Supporting Second-Grade Readers at the Beginning of the School Year

Second graders begin the school year with a better understanding of the rules and routines of reading workshop. They have more experience with books and should be entering the grade at Fountas and Pinnell reading levels H–J. However, each student is unique. It's important to assess his or her abilities, because some children fall back a level during the summer if they've had little exposure to just-right books.

Students entering second grade have moved beyond books with patterns and are beginning to enter the world of early chapter books and books in a series. These types of books have stronger plots, more characters, more words and sentences per page, dialogue, and varying fonts. Although both types present more vocabulary challenges, they do have picture support and contain many sight words.

Additionally, second graders read a variety of genres and are better able to monitor for meaning. Their fluency has grown as they have begun to develop good phrasing. Students are able to relate to characters more, and they retell stories in greater detail by including story elements. They've moved beyond finger pointing and have begun to scan words with their eyes, as well as read in their minds.

Tyrie chooses a nonfiction level I book about spiders. He demonstrates mastery of most first-grade objectives (objectives A–E), and understands and follows the routines of reading workshop. He knows that photographs in nonfiction books help present more information. Tyrie uses print strategies to figure out unknown words, and he chooses books that are of great interest to him. Based on these observations and the objectives, Tyrie's teacher might choose to work on one of the following:

- Developing good book-talk skills, such as keeping your eyes on your partner when sharing ideas
- Retelling the information gathered from reading or photographs

Here's how a conference between Tyrie and his teacher focusing on partner work might go:

Ms. H: Good morning, Tyrie! Oh, wow! You're reading about spiders? Ugh—I hate spiders!

Tyrie: Really? They're so cool! I'm learning a lot from this book! Look at this page! Can you find the spider?

Ms. H: Um . . . oh, I see it!

(Ms. H points out the spider to Tyrie.)

Ms. H: I'm so glad you chose a book that interests you, and you can read it too! It's important to practice reading in books that are just right for us! We're going to have partner time in a minute. May I watch you with your partner?

Tyrie: Sure. My partner is Patrick.

(Ms. H signals the class to switch to partner time. Tyrie calls Patrick over to their spot. Patrick begins to show Tyrie his book about bears, but Tyrie is looking at the cover of his spider book.)

Ms. H: Hey, guys. I'd like to talk to you for a second. When it's partner time, we want to make sure we listen to our partner. One way to show we're listening is to look at our partner's face when he talks. Watch how I do that. So, Patrick, what were you saying about bears?

Patrick: Bears come in lots of colors. Here's a polar bear. He's white. And a grizzly bear is brown. See!

Ms. H: Tyrie, did you see how I looked at Patrick when he was speaking? That's what I want you to do. Patrick, show us another bear.

(Patrick shows a panda bear and talks about its colors, while Tyrie looks attentively at him and his book.)

Reading Conference Notes | Launching the Reading Workshop

UNIT OBJECTIVES | GRADES 1–2

1–2 Developing Skills

A. Understands and follows workshop routines (e.g., book choice, book handling, conferences)
B. Tells the story through reading the pictures and some words
C. Is developing good book talk skills (e.g., faces the speaker, takes turns)
D. Uses early print strategies (e.g., 1-to-1 matching, picture clues, letter-sound correspondence)
E. Chooses appropriate independent reading books

F. Builds reading stamina (reads through the entire period)
G. Identifies basic story elements (plot, characters, setting)
H. Begins to retell in sequential order using story elements
I. Shows evidence of comprehension through thoughtful predictions
J. Envisions parts of the story well (can see what is happening without the support of illustrations)

Date/Text	What the Reader Can Do	Teaching Point	Next Steps
Sept. 7 Hidden Spiders Level I	A B—looks at photos D E—interest and level	C—listen to partner (eyes on partner)	G—nonfiction retell (say what you learned)

Student: Tyrie

In the next conference, Ms. H will work with Tyrie in recalling information from his reading.

Portrait of Readers in the Middle of the Year

By the middle of the year, children have learned the routines and expectations in your classroom. They've probably had several different reading partners and have learned how to relate to different personalities. All students are better decoders who have a repertoire of comprehension skills.

SUPPORTING KINDERGARTEN READERS IN THE MIDDLE OF THE SCHOOL YEAR

Kindergarteners are in a transition phase at this point in the school year. They're ready to delve into just-right books. In fact, some students already may have begun reading these books, but most are about to start with reading Fountas and Pinnell level A books. They're moving away from simply telling familiar stories and using only pictures to help them decode toward reading books with patterns, sight words, and simple sentence structures. Students are also realizing that their spoken words should match the words on the page, and they're excited to show you how well they can read.

Reading at level A, Kayla knows some sight words. She uses pictures to help her determine unknown words. Based on these observations and the Building Accuracy and Fluency unit objectives, Kayla's teacher might choose to work on one of the following:

- Stating the pattern in the text
- Recognizing more sight words to build accuracy

Here's how a conference between Kayla and her teacher focusing on stating patterns in the text might go:

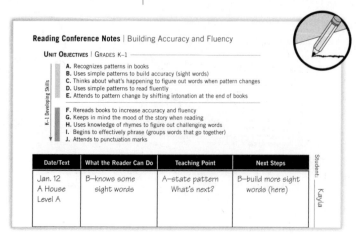

Reading Conference Notes | Building Accuracy and Fluency

UNIT OBJECTIVES | GRADES K–1

K–1 Developing Skills

A. Recognizes patterns in books
B. Uses simple patterns to build accuracy (sight words)
C. Thinks about what's happening to figure out words when pattern changes
D. Uses simple patterns to read fluently
E. Attends to pattern change by shifting intonation at the end of books

F. Rereads books to increase accuracy and fluency
G. Keeps in mind the mood of the story when reading
H. Uses knowledge of rhymes to figure out challenging words
I. Begins to effectively phrase (groups words that go together)
J. Attends to punctuation marks

Date/Text	What the Reader Can Do	Teaching Point	Next Steps	Student: Kayla
Jan. 12 A House Level A	B–knows some sight words	A–state pattern What's next?	B–build more sight words (here)	

Ms. B notes that Kayla needs to continue to build her sight-word knowledge.

Ms. B: Hi, Kayla. What are you reading?

(Kayla shows Ms. B her book, *A House*.)

Ms. B: Let me hear you read a couple of pages.

(Kayla begins to read, and Ms. B notices she knows some sight words, such as *is* and *a*.)

Ms. B: You remembered your sight words!

Kayla: I know *is*. It's on our word wall.

Ms. B: You're right! I see you're having trouble with this word. This word is *here*. We'll have to add it to our word wall soon.

Kayla: Thanks.

Ms. B: When I'm reading these books, I like to figure out the pattern so I know what's coming even before I turn the page.

(Ms. B takes out another pattern book and models how she notices the same words on every page.)

Ms. B: I think the pattern is "I see a . . . " Let me check the next page and see if those words are there.

(Ms. B turns the page.)

Kayla: There they are!

Ms. B: Can you figure out the pattern in your book? Let's read the first two pages together.

(After Kayla looks at the book, they begin to read together. Kayla starts to say the pattern as she turns the page.)

Kayla: I know it! It says, "Here is a . . ."

Ms. B: You're right! Next time, try to figure out the patterns in the books so you'll know what's coming next!

SUPPORTING FIRST-GRADER READERS IN THE MIDDLE OF THE SCHOOL YEAR

By the middle of the year, first graders tend to read books between Fountas and Pinnell levels E–G. The structure of these books no longer revolves around patterns. Their sentences are varied in structure and length. More dialogue occurs in these books, and a simple plot moves the story along. The type is still large, and pictures are still highly supportive to aid comprehension. Readers are no longer pointing to every word but are sweeping their fingers and eyes across the sentences to build fluency. At this stage, students are better able to use multiple strategies all at once to decode an unknown word and to read with greater expression. They continue to monitor for meaning and can self-correct. Finally, they're able to accurately retell the beginning, middle, and ending of stories.

Daniel reads at level G in the middle of his first-grade year. He has built his reading stamina and can read for more than 25 minutes at a time. He enjoys sharing the funny parts of his story with his reading partner. Based on the objectives of the Print Strategies unit, Daniel's teacher might choose to work on one of the following:

- Using a prompt to help him begin to retell the story
- Retelling the story in a few sentences (the gist)

Here's how a conference between Daniel and his teacher focusing on using a prompt to retell the story:

Mr. L: Hey, Daniel. I love *Poochie the Poodle!*

Daniel: Me, too. It's so funny. Look at this page. Suzie thinks she'll look like a poodle when she gets a haircut!

Mr. L: Yeah, that's really funny! I've never seen a haircut like that. You did a good job showing me your favorite part and telling me why you like it! What's this book about?

Daniel: Mmm . . . how the girl doesn't want a haircut.

Mr. L: Well, you're right. That does happen in the book, but good readers tell what happens at the beginning, middle, and end of a book. Let's try and say what the whole *book* is about: This book is about . . .

(Daniel glances at the pages.)

Daniel: This book is about how Poochie was hot. Poochie cut her hair, and then the girl thought she needed a haircut!

Mr. L: That's better! Try to remember to say what the whole book is about next time.

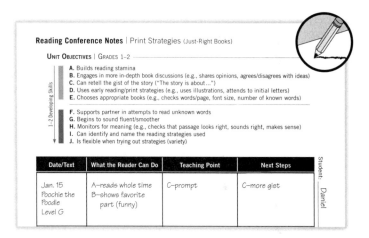

Mr. L wants Daniel to use a prompt to help him stay focused in his reading. This strategy will help Daniel's comprehension of the books he reads in the future.

Although first graders should be reading Fountas and Pinnell level E–G at this time of year, you may have some readers who are struggling to meet grade-level standards. Many of them will demonstrate the characteristics of kindergarten readers later in the school year. (See the section on Supporting Kindergarten Readers Late in the Year on pages 75–76.) These readers need extra support in building sight word vocabulary, knowledge of letter-sound correspondence, using picture supports, and understanding the patterns in these early texts to help build accuracy. For these first-graders, use the conference note sheets for Grades K–1 for the specific unit of study.

SUPPORTING SECOND-GRADE READERS IN THE MIDDLE OF THE SCHOOL YEAR

By the middle of the year, second graders are reading more difficult chapter books, around Fountas and Pinnell level K. They have a better grasp of how to read books in a series, and they talk more deeply about them. Using tools such as sticky notes and logs, they record their thinking more often. Also, students are able to decode ("word solve") using a diverse range of strategies and to carry the plot and characters in their minds over the course of several short chapters. The books second graders read tend to have more than one main character and several secondary characters. The characters tend to lead simple lives and face a main problem that they solve over the course of the book. Some of these books are broken into smaller chapters. Picture support is still present, but students must begin to make inferences based on the text. By now, they're reading silently and have build up more stamina.

Allie, a level K reader, enjoys reading The Littles series. Since she's been reading this series for a while, she can identify all the characters and feels she knows them well. Based on these observations and the objectives for the Character Investigation unit, Allie's teacher might choose to work on one of the following:

- Anticipating the actions of the characters by stopping to think: *What might they do next based on what I know about them?*
- Using sticky notes to help you stop and think

Here's how a conference between Allie and her teacher focusing on stopping to think to predict might go:

Ms. H: Allie, are you reading another Littles book? I guess you like this series and know the characters well.

Allie: I do. I picked this one 'cause it's about Christmas. I went to Florida for Christmas.

Ms. H: That must have been fun. Where are the Littles in this book?

Allie: They live in a big valley—it's Tom and Lucy. But their uncle, Uncle Nick, used to always be in Trash City!

Ms. H: Wow! You're really good at keeping track of the characters. You even know where they are in the story. Can you read a little bit to me?

(Allie begins to read on in her story. Ms. H notices that this is an appropriate book to use to work on predictions. She decides to prompt Allie to stop and think about what might happen next.)

Ms. H: Wait, Allie. It's so much fun when I'm reading and I know the characters well enough to guess what's going to happen next. Like right here—I'm thinking that Tom and Lucy might go on an adventure to where Uncle Nick used to work.

Allie: Yeah . . . I think so too. They love adventures!

(Allie reads on. Ms. H stops her.)

Ms. H: How about here? What do you think they'll do next?

Allie: They're going to get a ride to Trash City.

Ms. H: Great predicting! Let's read on and see if you're right.

(Allie reads the next couple of pages.)

Allie: See? I was right!

Ms. H: So, as you read on in the book, you can stop and tell yourself what the characters might do next. Then you can check your prediction.

Allie: I'll try that!

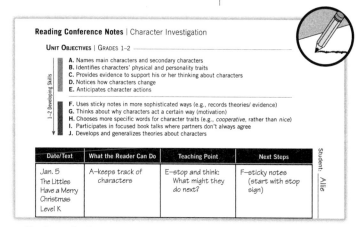

Ms. H can further encourage Allie to stop and think by using sticky notes. Eventually this will become a life-long reading habit.

Portrait of Readers Late in the Year

As the school year winds down, children have become better decoders and strengthened their reading in all areas, including accuracy, fluency, and expression. They're better able to explain their thinking to partners and small groups, and they can name the strategies they're using during their reading. By now, all levels of students are reading books in a wide range of genres and understand how to read these different genres. As their stamina has grown, they've become more independent readers. Students know how to shop for books. They understand how the library is set up, and they look forward to using it.

SUPPORTING KINDERGARTEN READERS LATE IN THE SCHOOL YEAR

Kindergarteners have moved from being nonreaders to reading easy texts. Confident about reading, they enjoy talking about their books. They're excited about moving to first grade and want to read harder books. By this point in the year, they know a lot of sight words and can recognize them in a text. They also can identify most of the letters in the alphabet and the sound each letter makes, which, along with support from pictures, helps them decode words. Kindergarteners can talk more clearly with a partner and have a better grasp of how to use patterns in a text to read fluently. You can expect most of them to end the school year reading at Fountas and Pinnell levels B–D. Books at these levels continue to have a pattern with substantial picture support and sight words, and simple sentence structures with concepts children are familiar with.

Bethany knows the routines for working with a reading partner. The teacher observes that she chooses a book quickly and decides to echo-read it with her partner. As Bethany and her partner, Tommy, read the book, they react to it. Based on these observations and the objectives of the Building Your Book Talk unit, Bethany's teacher might choose to work on one of the following:

- Talking about the pictures in the book
- Connecting the discussion to the text (staying on topic)

Here's how a conference between Bethany and Tommy and their teacher focusing on staying on topic might go:

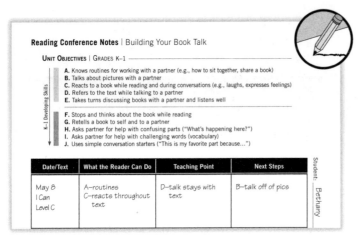

Reading Conference Notes | Building Your Book Talk

UNIT OBJECTIVES | GRADES K–1

K–1 Developing Skills

A. Knows routines for working with a partner (e.g., how to sit together, share a book)
B. Talks about pictures with a partner
C. Reacts to a book while reading and during conversations (e.g., laughs, expresses feelings)
D. Refers to the text while talking to a partner
E. Takes turns discussing books with a partner and listens well

F. Stops and thinks about the book while reading
G. Retells a book to self and to a partner
H. Asks partner for help with confusing parts ("What's happening here?")
I. Asks partner for help with challenging words (vocabulary)
J. Uses simple conversation starters ("This is my favorite part because...")

Date/Text	What the Reader Can Do	Teaching Point	Next Steps	Student: Bethany
May 8 I Can Level C	A—routines C—reacts throughout text	D—talk stays with text	B—talk off of pics	

In a future conference, Ms. H wants Bethany and her partner to be able to look more closely at the pictures and to talk about them in a meaningful way.

Ms. H: Hello, Bethany. I see you and your partner, Tommy, know where to sit during partner time. I'm so happy to see you two sharing one book.

Bethany: We're reading *I Can*. I'm telling Tommy all the things I can do. Do you know that I can feed my baby brother? He's one year old.

Tommy: I know how to play soccer.

Ms. H: You guys know how to do a lot of things, but when it's reading time, we want to talk about the books we're reading. Let's look at your book and see if there are things in there that you can do, too.

(Ms. H redirects their attention to the book and begins to read the first page.)

Bethany: I know how to button my pants, and she's buttoning her shirt. Look! I have buttons too!

(Bethany points to the button on her pants.)

Ms. H: Very good, Bethany. You told me something that has to do with the book. We want to try to always say something that sticks with what's happening in the book.

(The children read on, and Ms. H can hear them talking about how they are learning how to tie their shoes, which is the task featured on the page they're reading.)

SUPPORTING FIRST-GRADE READERS LATE IN THE SCHOOL YEAR

By the end of the first grade, children should be reading books at Fountas and Pinnell levels I–J. These books are the same ones that beginning second graders are reading. (See the section Supporting Second-Grade Readers at the Beginning of the School Year, pages 70–71.) First graders are just now becoming familiar with characters in a series. They're more self-aware of the strategies they've been using throughout their reading year, and they've mastered many reading skills well by now, including predicting, retelling, and making connections to the text. As they read silently, they're creating more mental images.

Joshua, who is reading a series of books, makes plans with his partner about what they should do at the start of reading workshop. They work together to agree on a plan and follow it. Based on the observations and the objectives for the Reading Centers unit, Joshua's teacher might choose to work on one of the following:

- Developing a theory about the character
- Providing evidence from the text to prove theories about the character
- Sharing evidence with a partner

Here's how a conference between Joshua and his teacher focusing on developing a theory about a character might go:

Mr. L: How's your reading going today, Joshua?

Joshua: Great! I love Henry and Mudge. I've read six of them already!

Mr. L: That's wonderful, Joshua! I can see that you know how to read this series well.

(Joshua begins reading the book to himself. Mr. L lets him read for a little while as he takes out *Henry and Mudge: The First Book*.)

Mr. L: So, Joshua, what can you tell me about Henry and Mudge's friendship?

(Joshua begins to retell the whole story of *Henry and Mudge in the Sparkle Days*.)

Mr. L: You certainly know what happens in this book, but I'd like us to try to think about something new. Good readers try to come up with ideas about the characters when they're reading. Henry and Mudge are friends, right?

Joshua: Yes. Best friends.

Mr. L: Well, let's think about their friendship in the first book.

(Mr. L shows Joshua *Henry and Mudge: The First Book*.)

Mr. L: I love this book. I remember how upset Henry and Mudge were when they were apart. I think friends like to stick together.

Joshua: Definitely.

Mr. L: Now, let's look at your book. What can you say about friendship in this book? Any ideas?

Joshua: Well, they both couldn't wait for it to snow so they could do lots of things outside. Friends like to play together.

Mr. L: Excellent, Joshua. Keep trying to think of ideas about friendship when you read books about friends.

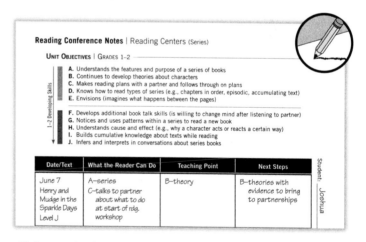

Mr. L notes that Joshua and his partner still need to have deeper conversations about their ideas.

SUPPORTING SECOND-GRADER READERS LATE IN THE SCHOOL YEAR

By the end of second grade, readers are truly independent. They read in their minds, and they can read for long periods of time. They're starting to master harder comprehension skills, such as envisioning, inferring, interpreting, critiquing, and evaluating. They're also able to set more of a purpose for their reading. For instance, you might hear children say that they're reading to learn about a topic of interest. Their vocabulary has increased and so has their ability to use strategies for comprehending unknown words. Many of the books children are reading are Fountas and Pinnell level L or M, and contain idioms or other phrases they've never heard before, but students are able to use context clues to help them determine the meaning of these expressions. These books are getting longer and more complex, requiring these readers to accumulate the text and synthesize what is happening. The plot often shows time shifts with flashbacks or fast forwards so students must keep track of the sequence of events. As the books increase in length, there is much less picture support. Finally, students tend to do more writing as they are reading to record their thinking.

Darnell enjoys reading level K magazines and books about space. His teacher has used the *Safari* magazines in the past during shared reading, so Darnell understands how the layout of a magazine functions. He's able to gather information from the photographs and the text and to name the various text features in the magazine. Based on these observations and the objectives for the Nonfiction Reading Strategies unit, Darnell's teacher might choose to work on one of the following:

- Accumulating knowledge about the topic of space by using a KWL chart
- Continuing to add to the KWL chart as you read on and gather further information

Here's how a conference between Darnell and his teacher focusing on using a KWL chart to accumulate knowledge might go:

Ms. H: You're reading a *Safari* magazine?

Darnell: Yes, Ms. H. I'm learning about the different planets. Look at all the things inside this magazine. There's even a play!

Ms. H: Wow! I love how you know exactly what you'll find in the magazine! Can you show me how you're keeping track of all the things you're learning?

Darnell: Uh . . . well, I haven't been using my sticky notes.

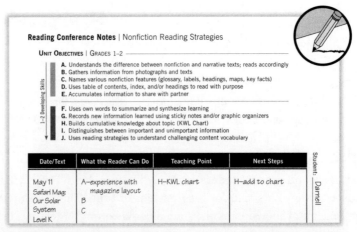

Ms. H introduces the KWL chart for Darnell to record information he knows, pose new questions, and seek answers. He'll be able to add to this chart in future readings.

Ms. H: I have a better idea. When I'm learning about a new topic, I sometimes try to remember what I already know about it to help me get started in my reading. I keep track of everything on a chart, called a KWL chart. Here's what a KWL chart looks like.

(Ms. H shows Darnell a blank KWL chart that he can use.)

Darnell: What do I do with this?

Ms. H: You see right here, where it says "K"? You can list a few things you already know about the solar system here. Then under "W" you can record some questions you want to find answers to. Then, as you're reading and learning new facts, you write the answers under the "L" section.

Darnell: Okay.

(Darnell starts filling in the KWL chart. As Ms. H walks away, Darnell has already recorded two things he knows about the solar system under the "K" section.)

No classroom is composed of a homogeneous group of students who consistently progress at the same pace through the school year. Some students will achieve grade-level expectations. A few will need ongoing support to reach these goals, while others will be ready to meet additional academic challenges. Recording your students' advances on your conference notes will allow you differentiate the assessment in your reading workshop so you'll be able to meet the needs of all your children at all times during the year.

Chapter 5

Improving Assessment, Planning, and Teaching With Data-Collection Tools

"The information that we gather about children comes from three interrelated sources. First, we watch children while they are learning; second, we talk to them while they are learning; and third, we gather together the products or artifacts of their learning. These are the three fundamental sources of information: observations, interactions, and artifacts. By carefully blending these three sources of information, we can construct a better understanding of the needs, interests, and abilities of our students, and then, use these understandings to make decisions about the learning experiences we need to provide in our classrooms."

FRANK SERAFINI (2001), *THE READING WORKSHOP: CREATING SPACE FOR READERS*

Before beginning any unit, planning is key. It's important to reflect on previous units of study, think about units to come, and consider student successes and difficulties.

In this chapter you will find answers to the following questions:

- What tools might help me plan my own units, and what kind of data can I collect with them?
- How might I use checklists within my own classroom to support reading workshop?
- How can my conference notes help me confer with the readers in my classroom next time?
- How can my assessments inform small-group instruction?
- How can my conference notes assist me in planning strategy lessons?

Making the Most of the Data You Collect

The information you collect from conferences can be very useful for planning your curriculum and instruction. As you look over your notes periodically, you may notice patterns within your classroom. These patterns can help you guide upcoming lessons and target areas where students need the most support. Several tools can help you collect and organize this data: the Reading Conference Notes sheet, different versions of the Planning Form sheet, and the Class Checklist sheet. (You'll find these forms on the companion CD and in the Appendix on pages 105–142.) We've introduced these tools in previous chapters and will explore them more here.

READING CONFERENCE NOTES SHEETS

The Reading Conference Notes sheets are designed to help you take shorthand, easy-to-review notes that allow you to track objectives for the entire year, unit by unit. Because the objectives you teach may change based on the needs of the students within your classroom, it's helpful to reflect on the goals of the previous unit before you begin a new one. Ask yourself the following question: *Have students met the goals I set for them?* If they still have not mastered some skills, you may want to revise your Reading Conference Notes sheet for the next unit to include these skills in the Unit Objectives list at the top of each sheet. You may also think about additional objectives you'd like to accomplish during a unit of study and add these to the list. This will guide you in developing the appropriate set of skills for the unit objectives.

The blank Reading Conference Notes templates shown below are ready to be filled in and can serve as a tool for you to develop student-specific goals for your units of study and create units we haven't addressed. You can also

**Reading Conference Notes
for Grades K-1**
Print From CD/Copy From Appendix,
page 122

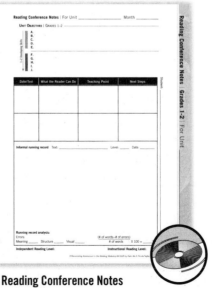

**Reading Conference Notes
for Grades 1-2**
Print From CD/Copy From Appendix,
page 123

differentiate or level the goals to meet the specific needs of your students. For example, a first grader who never attended kindergarten may need a simpler goal. You may wish to start her off with goals that represent reading-readiness skills, such as turning pages and holding the book the right way, while your more proficient readers are working on more difficult decoding skills.

Planning a Unit sheet
Print From CD

PLANNING FORMS

Different planning forms can assist you in preparing a unit of your own creation: Planning a Unit, Planning a Mini-Lesson, and Strategy Group Sheet.

As you plan a new unit, take a few moments to analyze how successful your students have been at mastering the previous unit's objectives. Ask yourself the following questions: *What went well during my last unit of study? Which goals did students struggle to accomplish? Which objectives do students need more practice in?*

On the Planning a Unit form, list your reading objectives for the next unit of study in order of increasing difficulty, and then use the notes on your planning sheet to help you complete a blank Reading Conference Notes sheet. Your unit of study will go much more smoothly as a result. At left is a sample of a planning sheet filled out by a kindergarten teacher.

For a discussion of using the Planning a Mini-Lesson sheet, see page 92. See pages 85–88 for information on the Strategy Group Sheet planning form.

A planning form helps teachers to map out the reading curriculum at a quick glance. Teachers can also be reflective and improve their teaching in the following months to come.

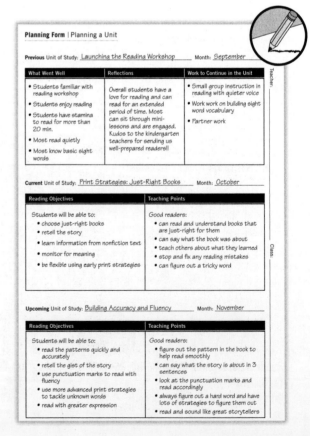

CLASS CHECKLIST SHEET

Looking at 20 or more conference note sheets can be over-whelming and confusing. It's also difficult to carry so many forms around with you, which is why Class Checklist sheets can become a helpful organizational tool. The checklist helps you keep track of how the class is doing as a whole, and it high-lights patterns of learning within your classroom. This data will enable you to differentiate lessons to meet all students' needs. The blank Class Checklist templates shown here may be filled in with objectives for units you've created to meet specific stu-dent needs. (Refer to Chapter 1, pages 19–21 for more informa-tion on how to use checklists successfully in your classroom.)

Using Your Notes for Future Conferences

Before you start to confer with a child, look at the last few Reading Conference Notes sheets you've completed for that student.

Look over the teaching points section, and notice whether the student is now successfully implementing the objectives you taught in your teaching point. If, in fact, this young reader is meet-ing those objectives, compliment him or her on successfully doing so. If difficulties are still apparent, you may need to reteach the skill during the next conference. You may also decide on teaching points for your next conference with this student by looking at the notes you've made in the Next Steps section. Any objectives that the student has not yet mastered can become future teaching points during conference time. Of course, the student's current reading will also serve as a guide for future conferences.

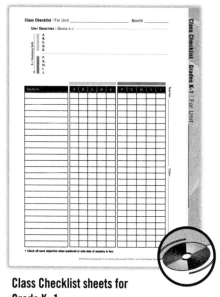

Class Checklist sheets for Grade K–1
Print From CD/Copy From Appendix, page 141

Class Checklist sheets for Grade 1–2
Print From CD/Copy From Appendix, page 142

The teacher glances at her previous conference notes on this student to help guide her conference.

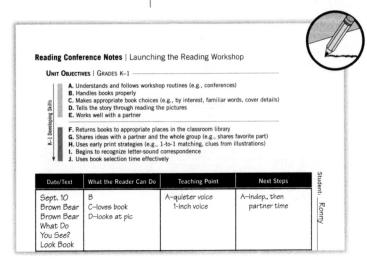

Reading Conference Notes | Launching the Reading Workshop

UNIT OBJECTIVES | GRADES K–1

K–1 Developing Skills

A. Understands and follows workshop routines (e.g., conferences)
B. Handles books properly
C. Makes appropriate book choices (e.g., by interest, familiar words, cover details)
D. Tells the story through reading the pictures
E. Works well with a partner

F. Returns books to appropriate places in the classroom library
G. Shares ideas with a partner and the whole group (e.g., shares favorite part)
H. Uses early print strategies (e.g., 1-to-1 matching, clues from illustrations)
I. Begins to recognize letter-sound correspondence
J. Uses book selection time effectively

Date/Text	What the Reader Can Do	Teaching Point	Next Steps
Sept. 10 Brown Bear Brown Bear What Do You See? Look Book	B C—loves book D—looks at pic	A—quieter voice 1-inch voice	A—indep., then partner time

Student: Ronny

Ronny still needs some help with objective A, so his teacher will probably work with him on independent reading followed by partner reading.

Let's put conferring preparation in action and prepare for a future conference with Ronny, a kindergartener, who was reading *Brown Bear, Brown Bear, What Do You See?* during the launch unit of reading workshop (See Chapter 4: Supporting Kindergarten Readers at the Beginning of the School Year, pages 67–68). A glance at Ronny's September 10 Reading Conference Notes sheet can give his teacher an indication of what to focus on for the next conference.

Ronny had difficulty reading in a quiet, 1-inch reading voice (A). It's important to notice how he's moving towards mastery of this skill before you begin your conference with him. A glance at Ronny's September 10 Reading Conference Notes sheet can give his teacher an indication of what to focus on in the next conference.

If Ronny is reading more quietly, the teacher may want to compliment his progress and move on to teaching him how to read by himself and then with a partner as previously noted in the Next Steps section. If Ronny is still struggling to read with a one-inch voice, the teacher may wish to revisit this teaching point, for example, by calling on other students who read with quiet voices to help model this skill.

You may also want to consult your Class Checklist sheet before making any conferring decisions. The sample below is for class K-101, Ronny's kindergarten class.

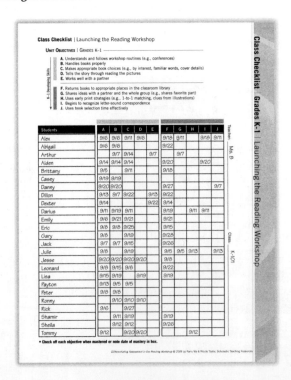

Class Checklist | Launching the Reading Workshop

UNIT OBJECTIVES | GRADES K–1

K–1 Developing Skills

A. Understands and follows workshop routines (e.g., conferences)
B. Handles books properly
C. Makes appropriate book choices (e.g., by interest, familiar words, cover details)
D. Tells the story through reading the pictures
E. Works well with a partner

F. Returns books to appropriate places in the classroom library
G. Shares ideas with a partner and the whole group (e.g., shares favorite part)
H. Uses early print strategies (e.g., 1-to-1 matching, clues from illustrations)
I. Begins to recognize letter-sound correspondence
J. Uses book selection time effectively

Students	A	B	C	D	E	F	G	H	I	J
Alex	9/6	9/6	9/11	9/6		9/18	9/11		9/18	9/11
Abigail	9/6	9/6				9/22				
Arthur		9/7	9/14		9/7		9/7			
Alden	9/14	9/14	9/14			9/20		9/20		
Brittany	9/5		9/11			9/18				
Casey	9/19	9/19								
Danny	9/20	9/20				9/27				9/7
Dillon	9/13	9/7	9/22		9/13	9/22				
Dexter	9/14				9/22	9/14				
Darius	9/11	9/19	9/11			9/19		9/11	9/11	
Emily	9/6	9/21	9/21			9/21				
Eric	9/8	9/8	9/25			9/15				
Gary	9/8		9/19			9/28				
Jack	9/7	9/7	9/16			9/26				
Julie	9/8		9/19			9/5	9/5	9/13		9/13
Jesse	9/20	9/20	9/20	9/20		9/8				
Leonard	9/8	9/15	9/8			9/22				
Lisa	9/15	9/19		9/19		9/19				
Payton	9/13	9/5	9/5							
Peter	9/8	9/8								
Ronny		9/10	9/10	9/10						
Rick	9/6		9/27							
Shamir		9/11	9/19			9/19				
Sheila		9/12	9/12			9/26				
Tommy	9/12		9/20	9/20				9/12		

Teacher: Ms. B

Class: K-101

• Check off each objective when mastered or note date of mastery in box.

Differentiating Assessment in the Reading Workshop © 2009 by Patti Ma & Nicole Taitler, Scholastic Teaching Resources

Class Checklist | Grades K–1 | Launching the Reading Workshop

The Class Checklist shows clearly which objectives students are having difficulty mastering.

Class K-101's checklist sheet for September's reading unit indicates that Ronny isn't the only student in the class experiencing workshop routine difficulties. Since most of the class is struggling with this skill, the teacher might find it helpful to teach a small-group strategy lesson on this topic. Addressing these skills with the whole class can save valuable conferring time. If Ronny still struggles with the workshop routine after the rest of the class is beginning to master it, his teacher may wish to revisit this objective during conference time.

Using Your Notes for Small-Group Instruction

When a handful of children in your class is not mastering a particular objective or is struggling with the same reading skill, you can fit small-group work into the independent reading time of your workshop, allowing 10 to 15 minutes for a group of three to six children. Although you won't be able to confer with as many individuals on the days that you do small-group work, this instruction will serve as conference time for the children in your group.

Two types of small-group instruction take place during reading workshop: strategy groups for work on specific objectives and guided-reading groups to detect any common reading problems.

Strategy Groups

A strategy group may be composed of students who read at a wide range of levels, but the focus is on a specific objective. Your Class Checklist sheets help you sort out students for grouping: when you notice four to six blanks spaces in a column, then it may be time to form a strategy group.

Another look at class K-101's checklist sheet reveals that small groups of students are having trouble with following workshop routines (A), handling books properly (B), and choosing appropriate books (C). These groups of children would benefit from meeting with the teacher in strategy groups to review materials, terms, and ideas you've covered in whole-group instruction and individual conferences.

When groups of children are able to move beyond the grade-level objectives, they can be pulled for strategy groups in which the focus is enrichment. For instance, some students in K-101 who have mastered objectives F–J may meet with the teacher to further enhance their mastery of all these objectives or to focus more intensively on one objective for an additional challenge. Using strategy groups can help you can differentiate instruction to meet the needs of your most talented readers.

Following your note-taking protocol for conferences, you'll use the Strategy Group Sheet shown here to take notes during strategy group sessions. These will serve as conference notes and help you keep track of which students you've met with and which skills

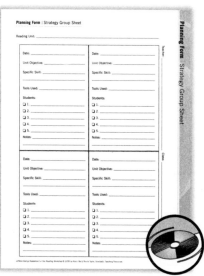

Strategy Group Sheet
Print From CD

you've targeted. After each session, mark the dates on the Conference Dates Checklist sheet for the students with whom you met. You may wish to indicate which students took part in small-group work with the abbreviation "SL" for strategy lesson.

As you take notes on the Strategy Group Sheet, remember to record the skill letter that you are working on in the space beside Unit Objective. You can then be more specific about the skill you are teaching. For example, if you are working on objective D, tells story through pictures, in the Launching the Reading Workshop unit, you may teach students how to identify the setting, characters, and events, or how to look at the pictures to guess what the characters might say. Keep in mind that you may have to reinforce the skill several times with the same group of children. Therefore, you may use different tools for each lesson. For instance, to teach students how to tell a story through pictures you may use sequencing picture cards, photocopies of pages from the text, different shared reading books and read-alouds, or puppets. Recording the tools used will help if you need to reteach and vary your approach.

Some objectives that will require small-group instruction are easy to antici-pate. For example, every year during the Launching the Reading Workshop unit, several first graders always need extra help with 1-to-1 matching or other early print strategies. Sally, Peter, Tim, and Cindy are typical first graders, and they are all struggling with pointing under words in the text for reading workshop.

Here's how a strategy-group conference focusing on 1-to-1 correspondence led by their teacher Ms. W might go:

(Ms. W calls four first graders to the rug for a strategy group. She asks them to bring their book bags and pencils. Each of their book bags contains their leveled books, "look" books (challenging books that students browse for enjoyment), and a few books of their creation, which were innovations from shared-reading big books. Ms. W brings small dot stickers and a student-made class book to the group conference. The rest of the students are reading independently at their seats.)

Ms. W: Hello, readers. You all have been working so hard during reading workshop by getting started right away and jumping into your reading.

Sally: Thanks, Ms. W! You know, I'm reading about a girl getting ready for school!

Ms. W: That's great, Sally. I called all of you to the rug because I want to teach you something to help with your reading. Readers make sure they pay attention to every word by pointing under it as they read. I noticed that you sometimes forget to do that, so I wanted to give you something special to help you remember. Look what I have!

(Ms. W shows them the materials she's brought with her to the rug.)

Peter: Oh! That's the book we wrote!

Tim: Yeah, and stickers! Cool! Can I have the red ones?

Ms. W: Yep, that's what I brought! All of you are going to get stickers, but first, let me show you what they're used for. Do you all remember the book we made? It was about how special each of us is. Now, I want to do something to help remind me to point under every word as I read this book. I'm going to take my pencil and draw a big circle under each word. Then, when I read, I'll touch each circle to help me point under a word. Watch what I do.

(Ms. W draws a circle under each word. Then she models how she reads by pointing at each circle.)

Ms. W: Now it's your turn to try it. Take out one of the shared-reading books we've made. Use your pencil to draw a circle under every word. While you're doing that, I may come over and ask you to read a page to me. Be sure to point to each word!

(The readers draw circles under the words, accurately marking each word. Ms. W stops to watch and listen to every student read. Their ability to point under the words has improved already!)

Ms. W: You guys did great! We can't write or draw circles in our classroom books, so I have these special stickers for us to place under the words in our books to help us with pointing. I'm going to give each of you a sheet of stickers to use. Go back to your reading spots, and place a sticker under each word. Then read your books and point under the words.

(Ms. W gives out the stickers and sends the children to work on the task independently. She notices the children are quickly getting to work.)

Ms. W prepared in advance for the strategy group. While she was planning her approach for teaching this objective, she filled in the top portion of the Strategy Group Sheet (see below), and this sheet became her lesson plan for the mini-lesson.

Planning Form | Strategy Group Sheet

Reading Unit: _Launching the Reading Workshop_

Teacher: _Wong_

Date: _9-16-07_	Date: _____
Unit Objective: _H-print strategy_	Unit Objective: _____
Specific Skill: _pointing to each word_	Specific Skill: _____
Tools Used: _dot stickers, books, sh. text, class innovation_	Tools Used: _____
Students:	Students:
❑ 1. _Tim_	❑ 1. _____
❑ 2. _Sally_	❑ 2. _____
❑ 3. _Peter_	❑ 3. _____
❑ 4. _Cindy_	❑ 4. _____
❑ 5. _____	❑ 5. _____
Notes: _____	Notes: _____

Ms. W notes the children she will meet with and the unit objective these readers need extra support in.

She continues to use the Strategy Group Sheet to record notes for the four students in this group. After Ms. W sends these students off to work, she confers with another student and then circulates around the room to check on how her strategy group is doing. If they are pointing at each sticker, she puts a checkmark next to each student's name.

Planning Form | Strategy Group Sheet

Reading Unit: _Launching the Reading Workshop_

Teacher: _Wong_

Date: _9-16-07_	Date: _____
Unit Objective: _H-print strategy_	Unit Objective: _____
Specific Skill: _pointing to each word_	Specific Skill: _____
Tools Used: _dot stickers, books, sh. text, class innovation_	Tools Used: _____
Students:	Students:
☑ 1. _Tim—rereads_	☐ 1. _____
☑ 2. _Sally_	☐ 2. _____
☑ 3. _Peter_	☐ 3. _____
☑ 4. _Cindy—self-corrects_	☐ 4. _____
☐ 5. _____	☐ 5. _____
Notes: _____	Notes: _____

Since all the students in the group appear to be showing mastery of 1-to-1 correspondence by pointing under each word, Ms. W can check objective H next to their names on the Class Checklist. If she wishes, she can also note the date of mastery.

Guided-Reading Groups

Children in the same guided-reading groups should be reading at the same level. Each group uses the same text when it meets so you should have multiple copies of books at different reading levels in your classroom. To allow children to practice reading a diverse range of work, these texts should also represent a variety of genres. Separate the books for guided-reading groups from your classroom library because you'll want students to "cold read" them in order to assess which skills students need to work on at each level. This "classroom guided-reading library" is for your use only. Some schools dedicate a small bookroom to guided-reading books, allowing teachers to borrow multiple copies of a leveled text.

You don't plan your teaching points in advance, as you do with strategy groups. Rather, you provide some support by introducing the text to students and pointing out vocabulary that may be challenging. As students read, listen for any difficulty they're having and make clear and concise notes on a Guided Reading Planning Sheet. If several children experience the same problem, it can become your teaching point at the end of the guided-reading group session. You can also ask questions to support your readers and have them complete a follow-up activity that relates to the text. Tell students to place these books in their independent reading book bags for continued practice and rereading throughout the week.

This sheet will help you keep track of whom you've met with, the book you assigned and its level, the objective you zoomed in on as you assessed students' progress, the supports you offered, challenges, and questions you posed. At the bottom of the sheet, you can record your specific observations about each reader. Indicate the dates when you met with guided-reading groups in the Class Conference Dates Checklist, using the abbreviation "GR" for guided-reading group.

Here's how a guided reading group led by Mrs. T might go:

(Mrs. T decides to pull a small group of kindergarteners together for a guided-reading session. On a Guided Reading Planning Sheet, she records the name of the text she's chosen, the date, and supports, challenges, and questions she'll pose about it. Since all these students are reading level B books, Mrs. T has chosen *Laundry Day* by Karen Hjemboe. She begins the conference by introducing the topic to the students.)

Guided Reading Planning Sheet
Print From CD

Mrs. T: Children, I have a special book for you to practice reading today. It's called *Laundry Day*. Have you ever helped your mom and dad do the laundry?

Adam: Yes! I help fold the clothes!

Jeremiah: Yeah, I put the clothes in the washing machine.

Shawnia: Me too!

Mrs. T: Great! Let's think about what you need when you do the laundry.

Jeremiah: Soap, clothes, a washing machine!

Shawnia: Yeah, and a dryer.

Mrs. T: What if you do the laundry outside of your house?

Shawnia: Like at a laundromat, like in *Corduroy*?

Mrs. T: Yes! Good thinking!

Adam: You need to put money in the machines.

Mrs. T: You remember a lot of important parts of doing the laundry. In this book, we'll see a little girl helping to do the laundry. Let's take a picture walk to see the order of the steps she takes.

(The children take a picture walk along with Mrs. T, noticing what's happening on every page.)

Shawnia: See, here's the dryer.

Adam: And before that, the washer.

Mrs. T: Before I give you these books, remember to look closely at the pictures to help you figure out what's happening on each page. Okay, when I give you the book, I want you to start reading quietly.

(Mrs. T hands out the books at staggered intervals to prevent choral reading. She listens as the students read and evaluates their reading behaviors on the Guided Reading Planning Sheet. Using these evaluations, Mrs. T determines which objective these students need to work on.)

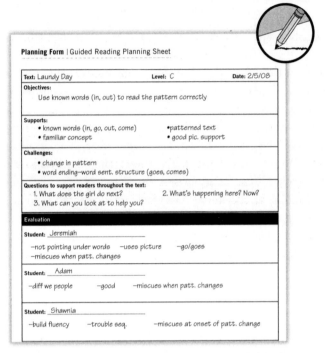

Planning Form | Guided Reading Planning Sheet

Text: Laundy Day	Level: C	Date: 2/5/08

Objectives:
Use known words (in, out) to read the pattern correctly

Supports:
- known words (in, go, out, come)
- familiar concept
- patterned text
- good pic. support

Challenges:
- change in pattern
- word ending—word sent. structure (goes, comes)

Questions to support readers throughout the text:
1. What does the girl do next?   2. What's happening here? Now?
3. What can you look at to help you?

Evaluation

Student: Jeremiah
—not pointing under words   —uses picture   —go/goes
—miscues when patt. changes

Student: Adam
—diff we people   —good   —miscues when patt. changes

Student: Shawnia
—build fluency   —trouble seq.   —miscues at onset of patt. change

Mrs. T notes that all three children in the group miscued when the pattern of the book changed. This will be her teaching point.

As students read independently, Mrs. T notices that all the students appear to struggle briefly with accuracy when the pattern changes, even though the words in the pattern shift are known words. She decides to make this her guided-reading objective. Later, Mrs. T has students complete a follow-up sequencing activity to reinforce the readers' understanding of the story—the ultimate goal for every reader.

This follow-up activity shows how well readers can retell the story.

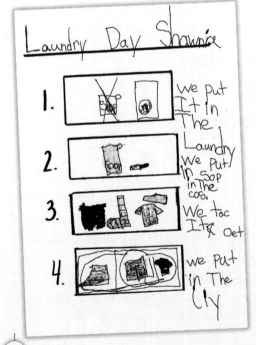

Using Your Notes for Whole-Class Instruction

Your decision to plan a whole-group lesson can be based on what you're noticing on your Class Checklist sheet. When you notice that most students have empty boxes for certain unit objectives and you have already attempted to check this objective, you'll need to reteach it at least once. Consider approaching the lesson in a different way. For example, if you used a mentor text the first time you taught the reading skill, the next time you may want to switch to another book.

When Mr. R, a second-grade teacher, looks at his Class Checklist sheet during the Building Accuracy and Fluency unit, he quickly sees that all the children are struggling to make their voices convey the meaning of the story (G). In the first lesson, he taught this skill by changing his voice to portray the different characters in *The Three Billy Goats Gruff*. This approach didn't work, and most students are still not changing their voices as they read. Mr. R considers what he might do to help students understand how to convey the meaning of a story better. He realizes that many children in his class are visual learners and decides to create a chart with the help of his second graders to show what each character in *The Three Billy Goats Gruff* sounds like. This chart will reinforce the idea that changing their voices to match characters will help make the meaning of the story clear. After this second lesson, he'll assess whether students are reading more expressively, mark the Class Checklist sheet, and determine whether to reteach the whole group, work with small strategy groups, or address the needs of individual students in conferences.

The Class Checklist sheet really helps you quickly decide what to do next. It serves as a quick reference tool and minimizes planning time.

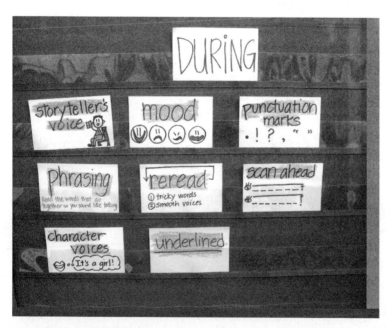

This pocket chart is filled with useful strategies that readers can use to help build fluency.

Planning a Mini-Lesson
Print From CD

PLANNING A MINI-LESSON SHEET

As you plan a mini-lesson, you want to be sure to consider all its components (see Chapter 2, pages 23–25.) The Planning a Mini-Lesson sheet below helps you address all the key lesson components and organize your ideas.

It provides several different options for how to approach your connection, teaching point, and active engagement. The completed planning sheet below shows how one second-grade teacher planned his lesson on teaching students how to use their voices to convey meaning when reading.

Now the teacher has a record of how he approached this lesson and how he can try a different connection, approach, or active engagement strategy if he needs to reteach the objective. The Planning a Mini-Lesson sheet reminds you of the many options you have at hand.

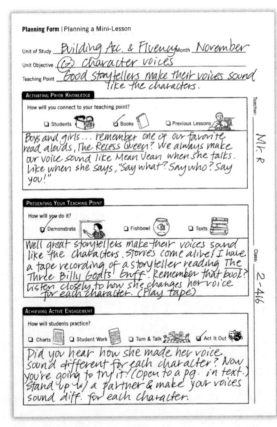

Mr. R has his students act out a part in the *Three Billy Goats Gruff* to encourage his readers to read like good storytellers.

Using these tools in concert will enable you to target key skills to teach and reteach in a timely way. Your conference notes and checklists are daily reminders of areas in which students are succeeding and need support. With this information, you can more effectively plan differentiated instruction for individuals, small groups, and the whole class.

Chapter 6

Using Your Conference Notes to Communicate About Student Achievement

"After conferences are over, we still have work to do."

CARL ANDERSON (2000), *HOW'S IT GOING?*

When you've compiled conference notes on the areas of growth and the skills that still need attention for the readers in your class, you will be better able to share this information with students, their parents, your school support staff, and administrators. It's important to let them know what strategies and structures the child has in place and which ones he or she needs to continue to strive towards.

In this chapter you will find answers to the following questions:

- How do I use my notes to communicate with my students?
- How do I use my notes to communicate with parents?
- How do I use my notes to communicate with school staff?
- How do I use my notes to communicate with administration?
- How might these conversations sound?

Using Your Assessments to Discuss and Support Student Achievement

When conferring is a consistent part of your reading instruction, students come to anticipate these conferences and pay attention to the notes that you take and share with them. In fact, these notes encourage accountability among them. They begin to realize that you will refer to

This student looks on as the teacher jots her conference notes. She knows what to expect.

your notes when you confer with the readers in your class. Students begin to realize that you will refer to your notes and check back to see if they are using the strategies that you've taught them.

Readers are more likely to try out the strategies when they think you and their reading partner are going to be listening to them. These compliments build accountability for the readers in your classroom: They'll practice reading smoothly because they expect that you and their reading partners will be listening to them. To help first- and second-grade readers remember the strategies you've discussed in a conference, you can place a bookmark listing these strategies in their book bags. In addition to encouraging students to continue practicing the strategies, the bookmark gives them ownership of their reading. You can change these bookmarks throughout the school year as you teach more strategies.

Whether you use a bookmark, sticky notes, a chart, or a just-right handprint (described below), all these tools serve as reminders and help you communicate your conference notes more clearly to students. The dialogue below shows Ms. C, conferring with Benjamin, a first grader, about his book choices. She notices he often chooses books that are too difficult. Having noted this area of need on Benjamin's conference note sheet, Ms. C decides to have him create a just-right handprint showing five different steps to check when he chooses a just-right book.

> **Ms. C:** Hi, Benjamin. What are you reading about?
>
> **Benjamin:** Uh, I think it's about spiders, but I'm not sure. See this picture— a spider is making a web.
>
> **Ms. C:** I'm glad you're using the pictures to help you figure out what you're reading about. That's really smart. But I notice you seem to be choosing a lot of tough books for your bag. I want to help you make the right book choices. We're going to make a just-right handprint to help you remember five things that help readers choose the right books. I'd like you to trace your hand on this sheet of paper.

(Benjamin traces his hand. Ms. C prompts him to think of five things to think about in choosing just-right books and writes one on each finger. When necessary, she refers him to a chart in the room that students have created about just-right choices.)

> **Ms. C:** When it's your turn to shop for new books, take the handprint out of your bag and look at it to help you in choose just-right books.

Using Your Assessments to Share Student Achievement Data With Parents

You can expect to meet with parents at least twice a year for parent-teacher conferences. However, you may meet with some parents more frequently if you're concerned about their children's reading. Conference note sheets help you remember specific skills they need to improve on. Parents will be encouraged when you share detailed observations about their child's reading.

You may wish to take out each child's current unit Reading Conference Notes sheet for his or her parents to refer to during your conference. You might even photocopy your notes for them to take home. One quick glance at the objectives at the top, and parents can easily see how many objectives are checked and which ones students still need to achieve. Since the objectives are listed in order of difficulty, parents can get a clear picture of where their child is currently performing on the continuum of developing skills for reading workshop, as well as where he or she is headed.

For parent-teacher conferences, you can tape a sample of a child reading and the conference

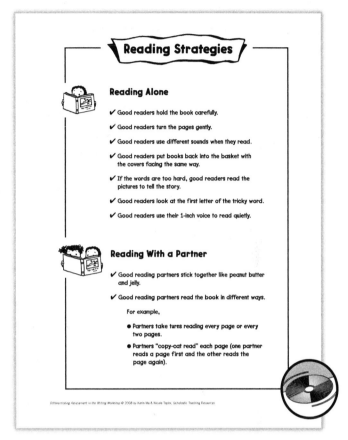

Print From CD

A send-home list of reading strategies gives parents ideas about how to help their child when he or she reads at home. Make sure the language is easy for parents to comprehend and matches the language you use in the classroom.

Nicole's | Classroom Notes

I've found it helpful to show parents any records I've made about their child's reading. These include reading logs that students have filled out, as well as graphic organizers, sticky notes, and follow-up activity sheets for guided reading. Sometimes it's difficult for parents to understand exactly where their child is struggling in reading since reading is an abstract activity. Concrete work products, such as written responses to books made on sticky notes and just-right handprints, can help parents better see where their child needs help. These work samples demonstrate the child's comprehension of texts. They also show parents that reading is not exclusively about decoding but that it also involves comprehension, fluency, and expression.

note sheets you've taken throughout the unit(s) to help guide your conversation. The dialogue below shows the skills that Ms. G, a second-grade teacher, has been working on with Luis.

(Ms. G meets with Luis's parents during parent-teacher conference night. Luis is an average reader who is able to decode well and tends to comprehend the texts that he reads. However, Luis lacks expression when he reads and usually uses a monotone voice.)

Ms. G: Good evening. It's so nice to finally meet you. Luis is a special student. He puts a lot of effort into his work. Let's sit down so we can talk. I'd like to show you the reading work he's doing.

Luis's mother: What level is he at?

Ms. G: Right now, he's reading level J books, which is right on target for second grade at this time of the year.

Luis's mother: Oh, that's good. When he reads to me, he knows all the words.

Ms. G: Yes, if you look at this running record I took on Luis, he's able to decode all the words. You see here, all these checkmarks are the words he said correctly.

Luis's mother: When can he move to level K books?

Ms. G: Well, Luis is still struggling to read with expression, which is an important reading skill. I've been having Luis tape himself reading so he can hear how he sounds. Would you like to hear a sample of him reading?

Luis's father: Oh, yes!

(Ms. G plays a portion of the tape. Clearly Luis's reading of the text lacks expression. His parents can hear Luis read the words with ease, but they recognize Ms. G's concerns.)

Luis's father: I see what you mean. We'll work on that at home. We can have him read to his little sister for practice.

Ms. G: Thanks. Your support at home will help Luis a lot. I'm sure he'll be moving to the next reading level soon.

Using Your Assessments to Share Students Achievement Data With Other Staff

You may need to meet periodically throughout the school year with support staff to determine the instructional program for students with special needs. Conference note sheets help you communicate specific concerns to resource room teachers, literacy coaches, ESL teachers, academic intervention staff, speech teachers, and other colleagues. If all the teachers in your school choose to use the same conferring tools, the shared format and note-taking protocols will make communication easier and much more effective. By consulting the conference note sheets and reviewing objectives that children have made progress on and those they still need to work on, support staff can better help these readers outside the classroom. They can also help you develop strategies that might help these children meet the objectives. For support staff such as instructional aides, who are not familiar with classroom expectations, these notes will help them better understand the big picture of the reading unit as well as the specific objectives individual children are working on.

Using the conference note sheets in mini-conferences with support staff, as shown below, makes it easy to collaborate and address students' key needs.

(Mr. J has set a brief meeting during his planning period with the speech teacher, Ms. Y, who is in the building twice a week to provide services. He wants to update her on which skills Maria is having trouble with during reading. Mr. J has noticed some articulation issues, which makes fluent reading difficult for her.)

Mr. J: Hi, Ms. Y. I wanted to get you up to speed on Maria's reading. I notice she has trouble saying some sounds and blends. My last reading conference notes with her show which words I was having trouble understanding.

Ms. Y: (Noting the specific items on Maria's conference notes sheet) We've been working on those sounds and blends. I'll do more articulation drills with Maria, and today, I'll send some information sheets home with her so her parents can help her practice, too.

Mr. J: Thanks. Now, let's take a look at . . . .

Using Your Assessments to Share Student Achievement Data With Administrators

In the course of the school year, there may also be times when you need to meet with your principal, assistant principal, or referral committee member(s) to discuss students in your classroom you feel are at risk, and may need to receive additional services, such as academic intervention, tutoring, or the resource room. It's important to have clear notes to show your administrators the areas of concern you have, as well as samples of student work. The more evidence you have, the more likely it is that your administration will be able to provide you and these students with the necessary support.

Occasionally, you may need to refer these children for additional services. You can attach copies of your conference note sheets or Strategy Group Sheets to your referrals, in addition to student work sample, to provide evidence that the student is struggling despite the reteaching work you've done. The following conversation is between a teacher and her assistant principal.

(Before the start of school, first-grade teacher Mrs. L meets with the assistant principal, Ms. P. The father of one of Mrs. L's students called the assistant principal because he received a letter alerting him that his son Alan might not be promoted to second grade. He claims that he cannot understand why his son may not be ready for second grade.)

Ms. P: Alan's father called me, very upset about the promotion-in-doubt letter!

Mrs. L: Let me give you some background.

(Mrs. L takes out her conference notes and planner, which lists the dates she spoke with Alan's father.)

Mrs. L: As you can see, I've met in person with Alan's dad on several occasions, and I've also had three phone conferences with him. Each time we discussed Alan's progress and his difficulties with reading. I've given him some suggestions for how to work on these objectives at home.

(As Mrs. L refers to her conference notes, Ms. P is very impressed.)

Ms. P: Wow! You are very organized! This documentation will be really helpful when I speak to Alan's father tomorrow. It will help support our decision to hold Alan back at the end of the school year—especially if the father continues to be combative. Hopefully, Alan will progress so we won't need to use all of this documentation, but it's always good to have.

Mrs. L: Please let me know how it goes with his dad tomorrow.

―――――――――――――――――――――――――――――――●

Conferring is a powerful tool. It will help you get to know each student in your class as an individual learner. You will be able to say with great confidence what each student can and cannot do. It will guide you to better instruction for the whole class, small groups, and one-on-one. When a teacher confers every day, the whole school community benefits. Conferring can help you create an ongoing support system that involves students, their parents, and school staff and administrators. Our goal is for every child to succeed, and conferring—when done consistently and purposefully—is an essential step toward reaching this goal.

References

PROFESSIONAL WORKS

Anderson, Carl. (2000). How's it going?: *A practical guide to conferring with student writers*. Portsmouth, NH: Heinemann.

Avery, Carol. (2002). . . . *And with a light touch: Learning about reading, writing, and teaching with first graders*. Portsmouth, NH: Heinemann.

Calkins, Lucy. (2001). *The art of teaching reading*. Portsmouth, NH: Heinemann.

Harvey, Stephanie & Goudvis, Anne. (2007). *Strategies that work*. Portland, ME: Stenhouse Publishers.

Meckley, Debra, Edwards, Lorraine & Stegeman, Deanna. (2008). *Reading with Strategies*. Upper Saddle River, NJ: Celebration Press.

Serafini, Frank. (2001). *The reading workshop: Creating space for readers*. Portsmouth, NH: Heinemann.

Taberski, Sharon. (2000). *On solid ground: Strategies for teaching reading K–3*. Portsmouth, NH: Heinemann.

CHILDREN'S LITERATURE

Adler, David A. (1981). *Cam Jansen and the mystery of the dinosaur bones*. New York: Puffin Books.

Adoff, Arnold. (2000). *Touch the poem*. New York: Scholastic.

Anno, Mitsumasa. (1977). *Anno's counting book*. New York: HarperCollins.

Avery, Dorothy. (1998). *Black and white*. Chicago, IL: Shortland Publications, Inc.

Avery, Dorothy. (1997). *Pass the pasta please*. Denver, CO: Shortland Publications, Inc.

Baker, Allen. (1999). *White Rabbit's color book*. London: Kingfisher.

Baker, Keith. Mr. and Mrs. Green series. New York: Harcourt, Inc.

Bang, Molly. (1999). *When Sophie gets angry . . . really, really angry*. New York: Scholastic.

Bertram, Debbie and Bloom, Susan. (2003). *The best place to read*. New York: Random House.

Brand New Readers series. Cambridge, MA: Candlewick Press.

Bridwell, Norman. (1963). *Clifford the big red dog*. New York: Scholastic.

Browne, Anthony. Willy series. Cambridge, MA: Candlewick Press.

Cameron, Ann. Julian series. New York: Random House.

Canizares, Susan & Chanko, Pamela. (1998). *First aid*. New York: Scholastic.

Capucilli, Alyssa Satin. Biscuit series. New York: HarperCollins.

Carle, Eric. (1988). *Do you want to be my friend?* New York: Scholastic.

Carle, Eric. (1988). *Today is Monday*. New York: Scholastic.

Carle, Eric & Martin, Jr., Bill. (1967). *Brown bear, brown bear, what do you see?* New York: Holt, Rinehart and Winston.

Cazet, Denys. Minnie and Moo series. New York: Scholastic.

Cohen, Miriam. (1989). *Will I have a friend?* New York: Aladdin.

Cosby, Bill. Little Bill series. New York: Scholastic.

Cousin, Patricia Tefft, Mitchell, Claudette C., & Porter, Gracie R. (1997). *I can*. Bothell, WA: Wright Group.

Cowley, Joy. (2001). *Dan, the flying man*. Auckland, New Zealand: Shortland Publications, Inc.

Cowley, Joy. (1990). *Going to school*. San Diego, CA: Wright Group.

Cowley, Joy. (1998). *Hairy bear*. Bothell, WA: Wright Group.

Cowley, Joy. (1986). *Ice cream*. Bothell, WA: Wright Group.

Cowley, Joy. The Meanies Collection. Bethell, WA: Wright Group.

Cowley, Joy. (1998). *To town*. New York: McGraw Hill.

Cowley, Joy. Mrs. Wishy Washy Collection. Bothell, WA: Wright Group.

Cowley, Joy, Mesler, June & Ross, Christine. (1997). *In a dark, dark wood*. United Kingdom: The Story Box.

Creech, Sharon. (2003). *A fine, fine school*. New York: HarperCollins.

Cutting, Brian & Cutting, Jillian. (1996). *In the air*. Bothell, WA: Wright Publishing, Inc.

Cutting, Jillian. (1996). *A day at school*. Bothell, WA: Wright Group.

Cutting, Jillian. (1988). *My friend*. Bothell, WA: Wright Group.

Danneberg, Julie. (2000). *First day jitters*. Watertown, MA: Charlesbridge Publishing.

Danzinger, Paula. Amber Brown series. New York: Puffin Books.

Dodds, Dayle Ann. (1999). *The shape of things*. New York: Scholastic.

Dr. Seuss. (1963). Dr. Seuss' *ABC: An amazing alphabet book*. New York: Random House.

Eastman, P. D. (1960). *Are you my mother?* New York: Random House.

Edwards, Pamela Dunkin. (2001). *Roar! A noisy counting book*. New York: Scholastic.

Ehlert, Lois. (1989). *Color zoo*. New York: HarperCollins.

Ehlert, Lois. (1989). *Eating the alphabet: fruits and vegetables from A–Z*. New York: Harcourt.

Feiffer, Jules. (1999). *Bark, George*. New York: Scholastic.

Fleming, Denise. (1991). *In the tall, tall grass*. New York: Henry Holt.

Freeman, Don. (1968). *Corduroy*. New York: Puffin Books.

Galdone, Paul. (1973). *The three billy goats gruff*. New York: Clarion Books.

Gamble, Danielle. (2004). *Poochie the poodle*. Chicago, IL: Wright Group.

Giles, Jenny. (1997). *Jack and Chug*. Crystal Lake, IL: Rigby.

Greenfield, Eloise. (1986). *Honey, I love and other love poems*. New York: HarperTrophy.

Grimes, Nikki. (2000). *Hopscotch love: A family treasury of love poems*. New York: Scholastic.

Guest, Elissa Haden. Iris and Walter series. New York: Scholastic.

Harwayne, Shelly. (1996). *What's cooking?* Greenvale, NY: Mondo.

Hess, Debra. (1994). *Wilson sat alone*. New York: Simon & Schuster.

Hoban, Lillian. Arthur series. New York: HarperTrophy.

Howe, James. Pinky and Rex series. New York: Aladdin.

Hjemboe, Karen. (2002). *Laundry day*. New York: BeBop Books.

Johnson, Stephen T. (1995). *Alphabet city*. New York: Puffin Books.

Jones, Drew. (2004). *Wake up!* Chicago, IL: Wright Group.

Keats, Ezra Jack. (1962). *The snowy day*. New York: Viking.

Kline, Suzy. Horrible Harry series. New York: Puffin Books.

Krauss, Ruth. (1993). *The carrot seed*. New York: HarperCollins.

Lee, Spike & Lee, Tonya Lewis. (2002). *Please, baby, please*. New York: Simon & Schuster.

Lee, Spike & Lee, Tonya Lewis. (2006). P*lease, puppy, please*. New York: Scholastic

L'Engle, Madeline. (2001). *The other dog*. New York: Books of Wonder Seastar Books.

Lobel, Arnold. (1979). *Days with Frog and Toad*. New York: Harper and Row.

Lobel, Arnold. (1996). *Frog and Toad treasury*. New York: HarperCollins.

Naylor, Phyllis Reynolds. (1994). *King of the playground*. New York: Aladdin.

Marshall, James. (1972). *George and Martha*. Boston, MA: Houghton Mifflin.

Marshall, James. (1988). *Round and round*. Columbus, OH: Newfield Publications, Inc.

Martin, David. (2002). *Piggy and Daddy play: Sledding*. Cambridge, MA: Candlewick Press.

Martin Jr., Bill & Archambault, John. (2000). *Chicka chicka boom boom*. New York: Aladdin.

McGhee, Alison. (2002). *Countdown to kindergarten*. New York: Scholastic.

McMullan, Kate. Fluffy series. New York: Scholastic.

Melick, Jane. (1993). *The gingerbread man*. Lexington, MA: D.C. Heath & Company.

Minarik, E. Homelund. Little Bear series. New York: HarperCollins.

Moore, Helen. (1996). *Beavers*. New York: Mondo.

Most, Bernard. (2000). *ABC T-Rex*. New York: Harcourt.

Munson, Derek. (2000). *Enemy pie*. Vancouver, BC: Raincoast Books.

Pallotta, Jerry. (1992). *The icky bug counting book*. Watertown, MA: Charlesbridge Publishing.

Parish, Peggy. Amelia Bedelia series. New York: HarperTrophy.

Park, Barbara. Junie B. Jones series. New York: Scholastic.

Parkes, Brenda. (1998). *Crunchy munchy*. New York: Mondo.

Penn, Audrey. (2006). *The kissing hand*. Washington, DC: Child Welfare League of America.

Peterson, John. (2001). *The Littles: Get trapped!* New York: Scholastic.

Peterson, John. (2000). *The Littles: Make a friend*. New York: Scholastic.

Prince, Sarah. (1999). *Playing*. Littleton, MA: Sundance Publishing.

Randell, Beverley. Baby Bear series. Crystal Lake, IL: Rigby.

Randell, Beverly, Giles, Jenny & Smith, Annette. (1996). *A house*. Crystal Lake, IL: Rigby.

Randell, Beverly, Giles, Jenny & Smith, Annetter. (1996). *Look at me*. Crystal Lake, IL: Rigby.

Raschka, Chris. (1993). *Yo! Yes?* New York: Scholastic.

Reading safari: Our solar system. New York: Mondo.

Roberts, David. (2003). *Dirty Bertie*. United Kingdom: Little Tiger Press.

Ross, Pat. (1997). *Meet M and M*. New York: Puffin Books.

Roy, Ron. A–Z mysteries series. New York: Random House.

Rylant, Cynthia. Henry and Mudge series. New York: Scholastic.

Rylant, Cynthia. Mr. Putter and Tabby series. Orlando, FL: Harcourt.

Rylant, Cynthia. Poppleton series. New York: Scholastic.

Sendak, Maurice. (1963). *Where the wild things are*. New York: HarperCollins.

Shannon, David. (1999). *David goes to school*. New York: Scholastic.

Shannon, David. (1998). *No, David!* New York: Scholastic.

Shaw, Charles G. (1992). *It looked like spilt milk*. New York: HarperCollins.

Slobodkina, Esphyr. (1996). *Caps for sale*. New York: Scholastic.

Spanyol, Jessica. (2002). *Carlo likes reading*. Cambridge, MA: Candlewick Press.

Taberski, Sharon. (1996). *Morning, noon and night: Poems to fill your day*. Greenvale, NY: Mondo.

Viorst, Judith. (1974). *Rosie and Michael*. New York: Atheneum.

Walsh, Ellen Stoll. (2007). *Mouse shapes*. New York: Harcourt.

Ward, Cindy. (2004). *Cookies week*. New York: Penguin.

Weber, Rebecca. (1998). *Balcony garden*. Chicago, IL: Wright Group.

Wells, Rosemary. Max and Ruby series. New York: Viking.

Wilhelm, Hans. (2005). *I hate bullies*. New York: Scholastic.

Willems, Mo. (2007). *I am invited to a party*. New York: Hyperion.

Willems, Mo. (2007). *My friend is sad*. New York: Hyperion.

Williams, Sue. (1989). *I went walking*. Australia: Omnibus Books.

Williams, Tom. (1998). *Before I go to school*. Chicago, IL: Wright Group.

Wood, Audrey. (1999). *Silly Sally*. New York: Red Wagon Books.

Wood, Douglas. (2005). *A quiet place*. New York: Simon & Schuster.

Worth, Valerie. (1996). *All the small poems and fourteen more*. New York: Farrar, Straus and Giroux.

Appendix: Reproducibles

Tip

To customize and save the files on the CD, you will need to download Adobe Reader™, version 7.0 or higher. This download is available free of charge for Mac and PC systems at www.adobe.com/products/acrobat/readstep2.

All forms are available on the companion CD

Reading Conference Notes | Launching the Reading Workshop

UNIT OBJECTIVES | GRADES K–1

K–1 Developing Skills

A. Understands and follows workshop routines (e.g., conferences)
B. Handles books properly
C. Makes appropriate book choices (e.g., by interest, familiar words, cover details)
D. Tells the story through reading the pictures
E. Works well with a partner

F. Returns books to appropriate places in the classroom library
G. Shares ideas with a partner and the whole group (e.g., shares favorite part)
H. Uses early print strategies (e.g., 1-to-1 matching, clues from illustrations)
I. Begins to recognize letter-sound correspondence
J. Uses book selection time effectively

Student: _____

Date/Text	What the Reader Can Do	Teaching Point	Next Steps

Informal running record   Text: _____   Level: _____   Date: _____

Running record analysis:

Errors:

Meaning _____   Structure _____   Visual _____

$$\frac{(\text{\# of words}-\text{\# of errors})}{\text{\# of words}} \times 100 = \_\_\_\_\_\%$$

Independent Reading Level: **Instructional Reading Level:**

UNIT OBJECTIVES | GRADES 1–2

1–2 Developing Skills

A. Understands and follows workshop routines (e.g., book choice, book handling, conferences)
B. Tells the story through reading the pictures and some words
C. Is developing good book-talk skills (e.g., faces the speaker, takes turns)
D. Uses early print strategies (e.g., 1-to-1 matching, picture clues, letter-sound correspondence)
E. Chooses appropriate independent reading books

F. Builds reading stamina (reads through the entire period)
G. Identifies basic story elements (plot, characters, setting)
H. Begins to retell in sequential order using story elements
I. Shows evidence of comprehension through thoughtful predictions
J. Envisions parts of the story well (can see what is happening without the support of illustrations)

Student: _____

Date/Text	What the Reader Can Do	Teaching Point	Next Steps

Informal running record   Text: _____   Level: _____   Date: _____

Running record analysis:

Errors:

Meaning _____   Structure _____   Visual _____

$$\frac{(\text{\# of words–\# of errors})}{\text{\# of words}} \times 100 = \underline{\hphantom{xxx}}\%$$

Independent Reading Level: **Instructional Reading Level:**

Reading Conference Notes | Print Strategies (Just-Right Books)

Unit Objectives | Grades K–1

K–1 Developing Skills

A. Prepares to read (e.g., previews cover and title, takes a picture walk)
B. Uses 1-to-1 matching by pointing under each word
C. Uses sight-word knowledge to read a story
D. Attends to the first letter when reading unknown words (gets mouth ready)
E. Uses illustrations to help decode unknown words

F. Chooses just-right independent reading books
G. Decodes unknown words by thinking about what's happening in the story
H. Rereads books in book bag many times
I. Begins to discuss books (e.g., shares favorite part and why)
J. Builds reading stamina

Student: _____

Date/Text	What the Reader Can Do	Teaching Point	Next Steps

Informal running record   Text: _____ Level: _____ Date: _____

Running record analysis:

Errors:

Meaning _____   Structure _____   Visual _____

(# of words–# of errors)

# of words   X 100 = _____%

Independent Reading Level: **Instructional Reading Level:**

Reading Conference Notes | Print Strategies (Just-Right Books)

UNIT OBJECTIVES | GRADES 1–2

1–2 Developing Skills

A. Builds reading stamina
B. Engages in more in-depth book discussions (e.g., shares opinions, agrees/disagrees with ideas)
C. Can retell the gist of the story ("The story is about…")
D. Uses early reading/print strategies (e.g., uses illustrations, attends to initial letters)
E. Chooses appropriate books (e.g., checks words/page, font size, number of known words)

F. Supports partner in attempts to read unknown words
G. Begins to sound fluent/smoother
H. Monitors for meaning (e.g., checks that passage looks right, sounds right, makes sense)
I. Can identify and name the reading strategies used
J. Is flexible when trying out strategies (variety)

Student: _____

Date/Text	What the Reader Can Do	Teaching Point	Next Steps

Informal running record   Text: _____   Level: _____   Date: _____

Running record analysis:

Errors:

Meaning _____   Structure _____   Visual _____

$$\frac{(\text{\# of words} - \text{\# of errors})}{\text{\# of words}} \times 100 = \underline{\quad} \%$$

Independent Reading Level: **Instructional Reading Level:**

Differentiating Assessment in the Reading Workshop © 2008 by Karin Ma & Nicole Taylor, Scholastic Teaching Resources

Reading Conference Notes | Building Accuracy and Fluency

Unit Objectives | Grades K–1

K–1 Developing Skills

A. Recognizes patterns in books
B. Uses simple patterns to build accuracy (sight words)
C. Thinks about what's happening to figure out words when pattern changes
D. Uses simple patterns to read fluently
E. Attends to pattern change by shifting intonation at the end of books

F. Rereads books to increase accuracy and fluency
G. Keeps in mind the mood of the story when reading
H. Uses knowledge of rhymes to figure out challenging words
I. Begins to effectively phrase (groups words that go together)
J. Attends to punctuation marks

Student: _____

Date/Text	What the Reader Can Do	Teaching Point	Next Steps

Informal running record   Text: _____ Level: _____ Date: _____

Running record analysis:

Errors:

Meaning _____   Structure _____   Visual _____

(# of words–# of errors)

# of words   X 100 = _____ %

Independent Reading Level: **Instructional Reading Level:**

Reading Conference Notes | Building Accuracy and Fluency

UNIT OBJECTIVES | GRADES 1–2

1–2 Developing Skills

A. Recognizes and uses a variety of text patterns to read fluently and accurately
B. Begins to summarize the main idea ("My book is about…")
C. Attends to more types of punctuation (e.g., ellipses, quotation marks)
D. Uses more sophisticated print strategies (e.g., blends, word families, medial/final sounds)
E. Builds expressive reading skills (sounds more like characters)

F. Uses print features to build fluency and expression (e.g., bold, italic, large font, underlined)
G. Shows meaning of story through oral reading that reflects mood, characters, illustrations
H. Scans print frequently to achieve fluent reading
I. Reads in a variety of genres using fluency and expression (e.g., fiction, poetry)
J. Helps a partner monitor for fluency and expression

Student: _____

Date/Text	What the Reader Can Do	Teaching Point	Next Steps

Informal running record   Text: _____ Level: _____ Date: _____

Running record analysis:

Errors:

Meaning _____   Structure _____   Visual _____

$\dfrac{(\text{# of words} - \text{# of errors})}{\text{# of words}} \times 100 = \_\_\_\_\_\%$

Independent Reading Level: **Instructional Reading Level:**

Differentiating Assessment in the Reading Workshop © 2008 by Karin Ma & Nicole Taylor, Scholastic Teaching Resources

Reading Conference Notes | Building Comprehension (Emergent Storybooks)

UNIT OBJECTIVES | GRADES K–1

K–1 Developing Skills

A. Chooses appropriate books and follows routines
B. Reads emergent storybooks from memory
C. Uses picture support when reading emergent storybooks and unfamiliar books
D. Understands basic concepts of print (e.g., cover, words, pictures, directionality)
E. Works well with partner

F. Thinks and states what characters might say or think
G. Builds reading stamina
H. Reads like a storyteller (e.g., uses voice, feelings, facial expressions, gestures)
I. Responds to books independently and with a partner
J. Begins using 1-to-1 correspondence to read words

Student: _____

Date/Text	What the Reader Can Do	Teaching Point	Next Steps

Informal running record Text: _____ Level: _____ Date: _____

Running record analysis:

Errors:

Meaning _____ Structure _____ Visual _____

$$\frac{(\text{\# of words} - \text{\# of errors})}{\text{\# of words}} \times 100 = \underline{\quad} \%$$

Independent Reading Level: **Instructional Reading Level:**

Reading Conference Notes | Building Comprehension

UNIT OBJECTIVES | GRADES 1–2 _____

1–2 Developing Skills

A. Retells accurately and sequentially using basic story elements (character, plot, setting)
B. Summarizes the main idea of the story
C. Stops and thinks about the book while reading
D. Records thoughts using sticky notes and/or reading notebook
E. Talks about thoughts with a partner and/or small group

F. Expresses thoughts about characters and their actions
G. Makes connections that build understanding of story (text-to-self, text-to-text, text-to-world)
H. Understands how chapters/scenes fit together
I. Shows understanding of difficult vocabulary using context clues (e.g., idioms)
J. Expresses a variety of ideas about texts (e.g., predictions, feelings, observations about characters)

Student: _____

Date/Text	What the Reader Can Do	Teaching Point	Next Steps

Informal running record Text: _____ Level: _____ Date: _____

Running record analysis:

Errors:

(# of words–# of errors)

Meaning _____   Structure _____   Visual _____   # of words _____ X 100 = _____%

Independent Reading Level: **Instructional Reading Level:**

Differentiating Assessment in the Reading Workshop © 2008 by Karin Ma & Nicole Taylor, Scholastic Teaching Resources

Reading Conference Notes | Building Your Book Talk

UNIT OBJECTIVES | GRADES K–1

K–1 Developing Skills

A. Knows routines for working with a partner (e.g., how to sit together, share a book)
B. Talks about pictures with a partner
C. Reacts to a book while reading and during conversations (e.g., laughs, expresses feelings)
D. Refers to the text while talking to a partner
E. Takes turns discussing books with a partner and listens well

F. Stops and thinks about the book while reading
G. Retells a book to self and to a partner
H. Asks partner for help with confusing parts ("What's happening here?")
I. Asks partner for help with challenging words (vocabulary)
J. Uses simple conversation starters ("This is my favorite part because…")

Student: _____

Date/Text	What the Reader Can Do	Teaching Point	Next Steps

Informal running record   Text: _____   Level: _____   Date: _____

Running record analysis:

Errors:

Meaning _____   Structure _____   Visual _____

(# of words–# of errors)

# of words   X 100 = _____%

Independent Reading Level: **Instructional Reading Level:**

Reading Conference Notes | Building Your Book Talk

UNIT OBJECTIVES | GRADES 1–2

1–2 Developing Skills

A. Stops and thinks about the book while reading
B. Records his or her thoughts using sticky notes and/or reading book/log
C. Uses ideas from sticky notes or reading log to contribute to partner talk
D. Asks partner for help with confusing parts/challenging words
E. Uses a variety of conversation starters, (e.g., "I agree/disagree...", "I think...")

F. Works well with small group for book talk (book clubs)
G. Listens to others and comments in response to their ideas
H. Refers to the text to support his or her ideas
I. Validates his or her thinking by explaining why ("I think... because...")
J. Looks back at sticky notes or reading log with partner to develop theories about characters

Student: _____

Date/Text	What the Reader Can Do	Teaching Point	Next Steps

Informal running record   Text: _____   Level: _____   Date: _____

Running record analysis:

Errors:

Meaning _____   Structure _____   Visual _____

$$\frac{(\text{\# of words} - \text{\# of errors})}{\text{\# of words}} \times 100 = \_\_\_\_\%$$

Independent Reading Level: **Instructional Reading Level:**

Reading Conference Notes | Nonfiction Reading Strategies

UNIT OBJECTIVES | GRADES K–1

K–1 Developing Skills

A. Understands the difference between nonfiction and narrative texts
B. Uses prior knowledge about a topic to get ready to read
C. Looks closely at photographs and illustrations to learn about the topic
D. Shares with a partner facts learned from reading ("I learned that…", "I never knew that…")
E. Reads with the purpose to find out information about a topic

F. Chooses books to gather information (choice reflects interest, answers questions about a topic)
G. Understands how to read different nonfiction books (cover to cover, in sections)
H. Notices and begins to read nonfiction features (diagrams, table of contents, captions)
I. Compares/contrasts information on the same topic across texts
J. Figures out challenging content words using a variety of strategies

Student: _____

Date/Text	What the Reader Can Do	Teaching Point	Next Steps

Informal running record   Text: _____   Level: _____   Date: _____

Running record analysis:

Errors:

Meaning _____   Structure _____   Visual _____

$$\frac{(\text{\# of words} - \text{\# of errors})}{\text{\# of words}} \times 100 = \underline{\quad}\%$$

Independent Reading Level: **Instructional Reading Level:**

Reading Conference Notes | Nonfiction Reading Strategies

UNIT OBJECTIVES | GRADES 1–2

1–2 Developing Skills

A. Understands the difference between nonfiction and narrative texts; reads accordingly
B. Gathers information from photographs and texts
C. Names various nonfiction features (glossary, labels, headings, maps, key facts)
D. Uses table of contents, index, and/or headings to read with purpose
E. Accumulates information to share with partner

F. Uses own words to summarize and synthesize learning
G. Records new information learned using sticky notes and/or graphic organizers
H. Builds cumulative knowledge about topic (KWL Chart)
I. Distinguishes between important and unimportant information
J. Uses reading strategies to understand challenging content vocabulary

Student: _____

Date/Text	What the Reader Can Do	Teaching Point	Next Steps

Informal running record   Text: _____   Level: _____   Date: _____

Running record analysis:

Errors:

(# of words–# of errors)

Meaning _____   Structure _____   Visual _____

# of words _____   X 100 = _____ %

Independent Reading Level: _____   **Instructional Reading Level:**

Reading Conference Notes | Character Investigation

UNIT OBJECTIVES | GRADES K–1

K–1 Developing Skills

A. Can name characters in books
B. Can list physical characteristics to describe characters
C. Thinks about characters in books
D. Shares thoughts about characters with a partner
E. Pretends to be a character in a book and acts out a scene with a partner

F. Retells what characters say and do
G. Attempts to predict what characters might do next
H. Makes personal connections to a character (e.g., "I have a sister too!")
I. Expresses feelings about a character (e.g., "I would want to be friends with her!")
J. Begins to name character traits (e.g., friendly, bossy, smart, kind, lazy)

Student: _____

Date/Text	What the Reader Can Do	Teaching Point	Next Steps

Informal running record Text: _____ Level: _____ Date: _____

Running record analysis:

Errors:

Meaning _____   Structure _____   Visual _____

$$\frac{(\text{\# of words} - \text{\# of errors})}{\text{\# of words}} \times 100 = \underline{\hspace{1cm}}\%$$

Independent Reading Level: **Instructional Reading Level:**

Reading Conference Notes | Character Investigation

Unit Objectives | Grades 1–2

1–2 Developing Skills

A. Names main characters and secondary characters
B. Identifies characters' physical and personality traits
C. Provides evidence to support his or her thinking about characters
D. Notices how characters change
E. Anticipates character actions

F. Uses sticky notes in more sophisticated ways (e.g., records theories/evidence)
G. Thinks about why characters act a certain way (motivation)
H. Chooses more specific words for character traits (e.g., *cooperative* rather than *nice*)
I. Participates in focused book talks where partners don't always agree
J. Develops and generalizes theories about characters

Student: _____

Date/Text	What the Reader Can Do	Teaching Point	Next Steps

Informal running record   Text: _____ Level: _____ Date: _____

Running record analysis:

Errors:

Meaning _____   Structure _____   Visual _____

$$\frac{(\text{\# of words} - \text{\# of errors})}{\text{\# of words}} \times 100 = \underline{\quad}\%$$

Independent Reading Level: _____   **Instructional Reading Level:** _____

Reading Conference Notes | Reading Centers (Concept Books)

UNIT OBJECTIVES | GRADES K–1

K–1 Developing Skills

A. Uses prior knowledge to get ready to read (e.g., reviews cover, title, pictures)
B. Uses pictures as a source of information
C. Uses concept knowledge to comprehend texts (e.g., numbers, letters, colors)
D. Identifies a common theme
E. Gains information about a concept from books

F. Understands how concept books are organized
G. Can predict what will be on the next page (e.g., "d" page follows "c" page)
H. Attends to initial consonant to help read words (e.g., "p" is for *puppy*, not *dog*)
I. Tells partner how books are alike or different
J. Can sort new books appropriately into existing concept book categories

Student: _____

Date/Text	What the Reader Can Do	Teaching Point	Next Steps

Informal running record Text: _____ Level: _____ Date: _____

Running record analysis:

Errors:

Meaning _____ Structure _____ Visual _____

$$\frac{(\text{\# of words} - \text{\# of errors})}{\text{\# of words}} \times 100 = \underline{\hspace{1cm}}\%$$

Independent Reading Level: **Instructional Reading Level:**

Reading Conference Notes | Reading Centers (Series)

Unit Objectives | Grades 1–2

1–2 Developing Skills

A. Understands the features and purpose of a series of books
B. Continues to develop theories about characters
C. Makes reading plans with a partner and follows through on plans
D. Knows how to read types of series (e.g., chapters in order, episodic, accumulating text)
E. Envisions (imagines what happens between the pages)

F. Develops additional book-talk skills (is willing to change mind after listening to partner)
G. Notices and uses patterns within a series to read a new book
H. Understands cause and effect (e.g., why a character acts or reacts a certain way)
I. Builds cumulative knowledge about texts while reading
J. Infers and interprets in conversations about series books

Student: _____

Date/Text	What the Reader Can Do	Teaching Point	Next Steps

Informal running record Text: _____ Level: _____ Date: _____

Running record analysis:

Errors:

Meaning _____ Structure _____ Visual _____

(# of words–# of errors)

# of words _____ X 100 = _____%

Independent Reading Level: **Instructional Reading Level:**

Reading Conference Notes | Shared Reading Texts

UNIT OBJECTIVES | GRADES K–1

K–1 Developing Skills

A. Follows reading routines well
B. Builds reading stamina (reads through the entire period)
C. Uses picture support to read texts
D. Remembers a text's storyline from read-aloud to support independent reading
E. Reads aloud with expression

F. Reads aloud fluently
G. Begins to point under each word (tracks print accurately)
H. Uses sight words to read accurately
I. Pays attention to the beginning of words to decode accurately
J. Self-monitors by checking whether what is read sounds right

Student: _____

Date/Text	What the Reader Can Do	Teaching Point	Next Steps

Informal running record   Text: _____   Level: _____   Date: _____

Running record analysis:

Errors:

$\dfrac{(\text{\# of words} - \text{\# of errors})}{\text{\# of words}} \times 100 = \_\_\_\_\_\%$

Meaning _____   Structure _____   Visual _____

Independent Reading Level: **Instructional Reading Level:**

Reading Conference Notes | For Unit _____ Month _____

UNIT OBJECTIVES | GRADES K–1 _____

K–1 Developing Skills

A.
B.
C.
D.
E.

F.
G.
H.
I.
J.

Student: _____

Date/Text	What the Reader Can Do	Teaching Point	Next Steps

Informal running record Text: _____ Level: _____ Date: _____

Running record analysis:

Errors:

Meaning _____   Structure _____   Visual _____

(# of words–# of errors)

# of words   X 100 = _____%

Independent Reading Level: **Instructional Reading Level:**

Reading Conference Notes | For Unit _____ Month _____

Unit Objectives | Grades 1–2 ——————————————————

1–2 Developing Skills

A.
B.
C.
D.
E.

F.
G.
H.
I.
J.

Student: _____

Date/Text	What the Reader Can Do	Teaching Point	Next Steps

Informal running record   Text: _____ Level: _____ Date: _____

Running record analysis:

Errors:

Meaning _____   Structure _____   Visual _____

$$\frac{(\# \text{ of words} - \# \text{ of errors})}{\# \text{ of words}} \times 100 = \underline{\quad}\%$$

Independent Reading Level: _____   **Instructional Reading Level:** _____

Class Checklist | Launching the Reading Workshop

Unit Objectives | Grades K–1

K–1 Developing Skills

A. Understands and follows workshop routines (e.g., conferences)
B. Handles books properly
C. Makes appropriate book choices (e.g., by interest, familiar words, cover details)
D. Tells the story through reading the pictures
E. Works well with a partner

F. Returns books to appropriate places in the classroom library
G. Shares ideas with a partner and the whole group (e.g., shares favorite part)
H. Uses early print strategies (e.g., 1-to-1 matching, clues from illustrations)
I. Begins to recognize letter-sound correspondence
J. Uses book selection time effectively

Students	A	B	C	D	E	F	G	H	I	J

Teacher: _____

Class: _____

• **Check off each objective when mastered or note date of mastery in box.**

Class Checklist | Launching the Reading Workshop

Unit Objectives | Grades 1–2

1–2 Developing Skills

A. Understands and follows workshop routines (e.g., book choice, book handling, conferences)
B. Tells the story through reading the pictures and some words
C. Is developing good book-talk skills (e.g., faces the speaker, takes turns)
D. Uses early print strategies (e.g., 1-to-1 matching, picture clues, letter-sound correspondence)
E. Chooses appropriate independent reading books

F. Builds reading stamina (reads through the entire period)
G. Identifies basic story elements (plot, characters, setting)
H. Begins to retell in sequential order using story elements
I. Shows evidence of comprehension through thoughtful predictions
J. Envisions parts of the story well (can see what is happening without the support of illustrations)

Students	A	B	C	D	E	F	G	H	I	J

Teacher: _____

Class: _____

• **Check off each objective when mastered or note date of mastery in box.**

Differentiating Assessment in the Reading Workshop © 2008 by Karin Ma & Nicole Taylor, Scholastic Teaching Resources

Class Checklist | Print Strategies (Just-Right Books)

UNIT OBJECTIVES | GRADES K–1

K–1 Developing Skills

A. Prepares to read (e.g., previews cover and title, takes a picture walk)
B. Uses 1-to-1 matching by pointing under each word
C. Uses sight-word knowledge to read a story
D. Attends to the first letter when reading unknown words (gets mouth ready)
E. Uses illustrations to help decode unknown words

F. Chooses just-right independent reading books
G. Decodes unknown words by thinking about what's happening in the story
H. Rereads books in book bag many times
I. Begins to discuss books (e.g., shares favorite part and why)
J. Builds reading stamina

Students	A	B	C	D	E	F	G	H	I	J

Teacher: _____

Class: _____

• **Check off each objective when mastered or note date of mastery in box.**

Differentiating Assessment in the Reading Workshop © 2008 by Karin Ma & Nicole Taylor, Scholastic Teaching Resources

Class Checklist | Print Strategies (Just-Right Books)

UNIT OBJECTIVES | GRADES 1–2

1–2 Developing Skills

A. Builds reading stamina
B. Engages in more in-depth book discussions (e.g., shares opinions, agrees/disagrees with ideas)
C. Can retell the gist of the story ("The story is about…")
D. Uses early reading/print strategies (e.g., uses illustrations, attends to initial letters)
E. Chooses appropriate books (e.g., checks words/page, font size, number of known words)

F. Supports partner in attempts to read unknown words
G. Begins to sound fluent/smoother
H. Monitors for meaning (e.g., checks that passage looks right, sounds right, makes sense)
I. Can identify and name the reading strategies used
J. Is flexible when trying out strategies (variety)

Students	A	B	C	D	E	F	G	H	I	J

Teacher: _____

Class: _____

• **Check off each objective when mastered or note date of mastery in box.**

Class Checklist | Building Accuracy and Fluency

UNIT OBJECTIVES | GRADES K–1

K–1 Developing Skills

A. Recognizes patterns in books
B. Uses simple patterns to build accuracy (sight words)
C. Thinks about what's happening to figure out words when pattern changes
D. Uses simple patterns to read fluently
E. Attends to pattern change by shifting intonation at the end of books

F. Rereads books to increase accuracy and fluency
G. Keeps in mind the mood of the story when reading
H. Uses knowledge of rhymes to figure out challenging words
I. Begins to effectively phrase (groups words that go together)
J. Attends to punctuation marks

Students	A	B	C	D	E	F	G	H	I	J

Teacher: _____

Class: _____

• **Check off each objective when mastered or note date of mastery in box.**

Differentiating Assessment in the Reading Workshop © 2008 by Karin Ma & Nicole Taylor, Scholastic Teaching Resources

Class Checklist | Building Accuracy and Fluency

Unit Objectives | Grades 1–2

1–2 Developing Skills

A. Recognizes and uses a variety of text patterns to read fluently and accurately
B. Begins to summarize the main idea ("My book is about...")
C. Attends to more types of punctuation (e.g., ellipses, quotation marks)
D. Uses more sophisticated print strategies (e.g., blends, word families, medial/final sounds)
E. Builds expressive reading skills (sounds more like characters)

F. Uses print features to build fluency and expression (e.g., bold, italic, large font, underlined)
G. Shows meaning of story through oral reading that reflects mood, characters, illustrations
H. Scans print frequently to achieve fluent reading
I. Reads in a variety of genres using fluency and expression (e.g., fiction, poetry)
J. Helps a partner monitor for fluency and expression

Students	A	B	C	D	E	F	G	H	I	J

Teacher: _____

Class: _____

- **Check off each objective when mastered or note date of mastery in box.**

Differentiating Assessment in the Reading Workshop © 2008 by Karin Ma & Nicole Taylor, Scholastic Teaching Resources

Class Checklist | Building Comprehension (Emergent Storybooks)

UNIT OBJECTIVES | GRADES K–1 ────────────────────────

K–1 Developing Skills

A. Chooses appropriate books and follows routines
B. Reads emergent storybooks from memory
C. Uses picture support when reading emergent storybooks and unfamiliar books
D. Understands basic concepts of print (e.g., cover, words, pictures, directionality)
E. Works well with partner

F. Thinks and states what characters might say or think
G. Builds reading stamina
H. Reads like a storyteller (e.g., uses voice, feelings, facial expressions, gestures)
I. Responds to books independently and with a partner
J. Begins using 1-to-1 correspondence to read words

Students	A	B	C	D	E	F	G	H	I	J

Teacher: _____

Class: _____

• **Check off each objective when mastered or note date of mastery in box.**

Differentiating Assessment in the Reading Workshop © 2008 by Karin Ma & Nicole Taylor, Scholastic Teaching Resources

Class Checklist | Building Comprehension

UNIT OBJECTIVES | GRADES 1–2

1–2 Developing Skills

A. Retells accurately and sequentially using basic story elements (character, plot, setting)
B. Summarizes the main idea of the story
C. Stops and thinks about the book while reading
D. Records thoughts using sticky notes and/or reading notebook
E. Talks about thoughts with a partner and/or small group

F. Expresses thoughts about characters and their actions
G. Makes connections that build understanding of story (text-to-self, text-to-text, text-to-world)
H. Understands how chapters/scenes fit together
I. Shows understanding of difficult vocabulary using context clues (e.g., idioms)
J. Expresses a variety of ideas about texts (e.g., predictions, feelings, observations about characters)

Students	A	B	C	D	E	F	G	H	I	J

Teacher: _____

Class: _____

• **Check off each objective when mastered or note date of mastery in box.**

Class Checklist | Building Your Book Talk

UNIT OBJECTIVES | GRADES K–1

K–1 Developing Skills

A. Knows routines for working with a partner (e.g., how to sit together, share a book)
B. Talks about pictures with a partner
C. Reacts to a book while reading and during conversations (e.g., laughs, expresses feelings)
D. Refers to the text while talking to a partner
E. Takes turns discussing books with a partner and listens well

F. Stops and thinks about the book while reading
G. Retells a book to self and to a partner
H. Asks partner for help with confusing parts ("What's happening here?")
I. Asks partner for help with challenging words (vocabulary)
J. Uses simple conversation starters ("This is my favorite part because…")

Students	A	B	C	D	E	F	G	H	I	J

Teacher: _____

Class: _____

• **Check off each objective when mastered or note date of mastery in box.**

Differentiating Assessment in the Reading Workshop © 2008 by Karin Ma & Nicole Taylor, Scholastic Teaching Resources

Class Checklist | Building Your Book Talk

UNIT OBJECTIVES | GRADES 1–2

1–2 Developing Skills

A. Stops and thinks about the book while reading
B. Records his or her thoughts using sticky notes and/or reading book/log
C. Uses ideas from sticky notes or reading log to contribute to partner talk
D. Asks partner for help with confusing parts/challenging words
E. Uses a variety of conversation starters, (e.g., "I agree/disagree...", "I think...")

F. Works well with small group for book talk (book clubs)
G. Listens to others and comments in response to their ideas
H. Refers to the text to support his or her ideas
I. Validates his or her thinking by explaining why ("I think... because...")
J. Looks back at sticky notes or reading log with partner to develop theories about characters

Students	A	B	C	D	E	F	G	H	I	J

Teacher: _____

Class: _____

• **Check off each objective when mastered or note date of mastery in box.**

Class Checklist | Nonfiction Reading Strategies

UNIT OBJECTIVES | GRADES K–1

K–1 Developing Skills

A. Understands the difference between nonfiction and narrative texts
B. Uses prior knowledge about a topic to get ready to read
C. Looks closely at photographs and illustrations to learn about the topic
D. Shares with a partner facts learned from reading ("I learned that...", "I never knew that...")
E. Reads with the purpose to find out information about a topic

F. Chooses books to gather information (choice reflects interest, answers questions about a topic)
G. Understands how to read different nonfiction books (cover to cover, in sections)
H. Notices and begins to read nonfiction features (diagrams, table of contents, captions)
I. Compares/contrasts information on the same topic across texts
J. Figures out challenging content words using a variety of strategies

Teacher: _____

Class: _____

Students	A	B	C	D	E	F	G	H	I	J

• **Check off each objective when mastered or note date of mastery in box.**

Differentiating Assessment in the Reading Workshop © 2008 by Karin Ma & Nicole Taylor, Scholastic Teaching Resources

Class Checklist | Nonfiction Reading Strategies

Unit Objectives | Grades 1–2

1–2 Developing Skills

A. Understands the difference between nonfiction and narrative texts; reads accordingly
B. Gathers information from photographs and texts
C. Names various nonfiction features (glossary, labels, headings, maps, key facts)
D. Uses table of contents, index, and/or headings to read with purpose
E. Accumulates information to share with partner

F. Uses own words to summarize and synthesize learning
G. Records new information learned using sticky notes and/or graphic organizers
H. Builds cumulative knowledge about topic (KWL Chart)
I. Distinguishes between important and unimportant information
J. Uses reading strategies to understand challenging content vocabulary

Students	A	B	C	D	E	F	G	H	I	J

Teacher: _____

Class: _____

• **Check off each objective when mastered or note date of mastery in box.**

Class Checklist | Character Investigation

UNIT OBJECTIVES | GRADES K–1

K–1 Developing Skills

A. Can name characters in books
B. Can list physical characteristics to describe characters
C. Thinks about characters in books
D. Shares thoughts about characters with a partner
E. Pretends to be a character in a book and acts out a scene with a partner

F. Retells what characters say and do
G. Attempts to predict what characters might do next
H. Makes personal connections to a character (e.g., "I have a sister too!")
I. Expresses feelings about a character (e.g., "I would want to be friends with her!")
J. Begins to name character traits (e.g., friendly, bossy, smart, kind, lazy)

Teacher: _____

Class: _____

Students	A	B	C	D	E	F	G	H	I	J

• **Check off each objective when mastered or note date of mastery in box.**

Differentiating Assessment in the Reading Workshop © 2008 by Karin Ma & Nicole Taylor, Scholastic Teaching Resources

Class Checklist | Character Investigation

UNIT OBJECTIVES | GRADES 1–2

1–2 Developing Skills

A. Names main characters and secondary characters
B. Identifies characters' physical and personality traits
C. Provides evidence to support his or her thinking about characters
D. Notices how characters change
E. Anticipates character actions

F. Uses sticky notes in more sophisticated ways (e.g., records theories/evidence)
G. Thinks about why characters act a certain way (motivation)
H. Chooses more specific words for character traits (e.g., *cooperative* rather than *nice*)
I. Participates in focused book talks where partners don't always agree
J. Develops and generalizes theories about characters

Teacher: _____

Class: _____

Students	A	B	C	D	E	F	G	H	I	J

• **Check off each objective when mastered or note date of mastery in box.**

Class Checklist | Reading Centers (Concept Books)

UNIT OBJECTIVES | GRADES K–1

A. Uses prior knowledge to get ready to read (e.g., reviews cover, title, pictures)
B. Uses pictures as a source of information
C. Uses concept knowledge to comprehend texts (e.g., numbers, letters, colors)
D. Identifies a common theme
E. Gains information about a concept from books

F. Understands how concept books are organized
G. Can predict what will be on the next page (e.g., "d" page follows "c" page)
H. Attends to initial consonant to help read words (e.g., "p" is for *puppy*, not *dog*)
I. Tells partner how books are alike or different
J. Can sort new books appropriately into existing concept book categories

K–1 Developing Skills

Students	A	B	C	D	E	F	G	H	I	J

Teacher: _____

Class: _____

• **Check off each objective when mastered or note date of mastery in box.**

Reading Conference Notes | Reading Centers (Series)

UNIT OBJECTIVES | GRADES 1–2

1–2 Developing Skills

A. Understands the features and purpose of a series of books
B. Continues to develop theories about characters
C. Makes reading plans with a partner and follows through on plans
D. Knows how to read types of series (e.g., chapters in order, episodic, accumulating text)
E. Envisions (imagines what happens between the pages)

F. Develops additional book talk skills (is willing to change mind after listening to partner)
G. Notices and uses patterns within a series to read a new book
H. Understands cause and effect (e.g., why a character acts or reacts a certain way)
I. Builds cumulative knowledge about texts while reading
J. Infers and interprets in conversations about series books

Students	A	B	C	D	E	F	G	H	I	J

Teacher: _____

Class: _____

• **Check off each objective when mastered or note date of mastery in box.**

Class Checklist | Shared Reading Texts

Unit Objectives | Grades K–1

K–1 Developing Skills

A. Follows reading routines well
B. Builds reading stamina (reads through the entire period)
C. Uses picture support to read texts
D. Remembers a text's storyline from read-aloud to support independent reading
E. Reads aloud with expression

F. Reads aloud fluently
G. Begins to point under each word (tracks print accurately)
H. Uses sight words to read accurately
I. Pays attention to the beginning of words to decode accurately
J. Self-monitors by checking whether what is read sounds right

Students	A	B	C	D	E	F	G	H	I	J

Teacher: _____

Class: _____

• **Check off each objective when mastered or note date of mastery in box.**

Differentiating Assessment in the Reading Workshop © 2008 by Karin Ma & Nicole Taylor, Scholastic Teaching Resources

Class Checklist | For Unit _____ Month _____

UNIT OBJECTIVES | GRADES K–1 ────────────────────

K–1 Developing Skills

A.
B.
C.
D.
E.

F.
G.
H.
I.
J.

Students	A	B	C	D	E	F	G	H	I	J

Teacher: _____

Class: _____

• **Check off each objective when mastered or note date of mastery in box.**

Differentiating Assessment in the Reading Workshop © 2008 by Karin Ma & Nicole Taylor, Scholastic Teaching Resources

Class Checklist | For Unit _____ Month _____

UNIT OBJECTIVES | GRADES 1–2 _____

1–2 Developing Skills

A.
B.
C.
D.
E.

F.
G.
H.
I.
J.

Students	A	B	C	D	E	F	G	H	I	J

Teacher: _____

Class: _____

• **Check off each objective when mastered or note date of mastery in box.**

 Differentiating Assessment in the Reading Workshop © 2008 by Karin Ma & Nicole Taylor, Scholastic Teaching Resources

For Unit _____ Month _____

Students	← ──────────── Conference Dates ──────────── →				

Teacher: _____

Class: _____

Differentiating Assessment in the Reading Workshop © 2008 by Karin Ma & Nicole Taylor, Scholastic Teaching Resources

Index